From the Eye of Ayahuasca

From the Eye of Ayahuasca © 2024 Jackie M. Guerra
Cuidado Editorial: Alegria Publishing
Diseño y Maquetación: @mckadamia
Ilustraciones: Jackie M Guerra
Diseño de Portada: @mckadamia
Cuidado de Edición en español: Paloma Alcantar
Cuidado de Edición en inglés:
Contacto: davina@alegriamagazine.com

ISBN: 9798991125048
Impreso en los Estados Unidos de América –
Printed in the United States of America

From the Eye of Ayahuasca

Journeys, realizations, and integrations with Ayahuasca (Aya)

By Jackie M Guerra

INDEX

Foreword:

Aya teaches us about the nature of reality. This ritual is more than just a psychological healing process. She teaches us about the nature of the universe, the nature of life, and, therefore, the nature of ourselves.

Glossary

Aya: Ayahuasca the medicine, the spirit of Mother Earth.

Ayahuasquero: A person that is trained to give and teach the medicine of Ayahuasca.

Kambo: An Amazonian monkey frog that is used to cleanse the body before ceremony.

Plant Dieta: A period of strict fasting and isolation where a healer learns directly from the plants and Maestro

Eckero: A sacred plant song sang by the ayahuasquero in ceremony

Shihuahuaco: An Amazonian tree known for its incredible strength that has the hardest wood on Earth, and is used for plant dieta to learn how to create boundaries.

Thy: A universal way of saying "me" or "my" without interpretation or expression of ego.

Agua Florida: Perfume of hundreds of Amazonian flowers made by a Shaman to bring in love and light.

Tobacco: The protector and holder of the space.

What Is Ayahuasca?

What Is Ayahuasca?

1.) Ayahuasca: A 4-6 hour dimethyltryptamine (DMT) experience; a night time medicine.

The ceremonial brew "ayahuasca" is a combination of two vines: *Banisteriopsis caapi* (also known as the ayahuasca vine or just caapi, which is not in and of itself psychoactive) and *Psychotria viridis* (also known as chacruna), which contains DMT. .

Caapi contains elements that allow other plants with hallucinogenic properties to become orally active. It also contains one thousand times the antioxidant level that green tea has, and is a natural antidepressant.

Caapi contains harmala alkaloids, which act as monoamine oxidase inhibitors (MAOIs). MAOIs have a variety of medicinal uses and effects, mostly as antidepressant medication. MAOIs neutralize the monoamine oxidase in your stomach, which allows DMT - the psychoactive ingredient in ayahuasca - to pass through your stomach into your bloodstream and, ultimately, to your brain. MAOIs also allow the neurotransmitters norepinephrine, serotonin, and dopamine to stay in the brain , causing a sensation of peace, acceptance, and euphoria.

MAOIs have a long list of medicine, food, and supplements that they can interact poorly with. Because of this, you should not take ayahuasca while on other medications (especially antidepressants), and you need to follow a strict diet that contains no sugar, salts, red meat, dairy, coffee, or cannabis for one week before your ceremony. The premise is to just be extra clean for a week.

The *Psychotria viridis* vine is referred to as *chacruna* in Peru and Brazil, and *samiruka* or *amiruca* in Ecuador. The word "chacruna" means "the mix" and refers to what is mixed in with caapi to create a non-ordinary state of consciousness. It may also be called "the mix" because it *mixes* your consciousness to make you aware of different aspects of life.

All forms of *chacruna* contain a high amount of DMT. DMT is found in most plants and mammals, but the presence of MAOIs in humans prevents DMT from having a psychological effect on us normally. When mixed with caapi, though, DMT crosses into the brain and bonds with serotonin receptors in the prefrontal cortex and the amygdala. This causes a classic non-ordinary state of consciousness with visual and aural hallucinations, a reduced fear and shame response, and increased empathy and interconnectivity. Unlike other classic psychedelics, DMT also binds with sigma-1 receptors. The transmembrane proteins, Sigma-1 receptors, are the overseeing messengers that modulate calcium signaling and other important cellular processes, which is currently being researched due to the sigma-1's relation to schizophrenia, depression, addiction, and cancer.

Ayahuasca requires intention. You get what you give with this medicine, insofar as the (i) prep week; (ii) the experience itself; and (iii) the integration thereafter.

In a typical four- to six-hour journey, a participant will experience varied emotional states and very often experience a sense of the divine. Sometimes the experience can be a bit more physical at first, depending on the participant and what they are working through emotionally and spiritually.– Ayahuasca is a powerful purgative, but don't let this intimidate you. It's not at all like consuming too much alcohol or having food poisoning. It is a different sensation altogether, and exceedingly healthy in terms of expelling the physical, mental, emotional, and spiritual trauma that we all accumulate throughout our lives.

Ayahuasca is the great maestra, the mother of all plants, la madre, la abuela. She guides you through multiple dimensions (at times blissful, at times very challenging), and leaves you right back at your doorstep, safe and renewed. It's magical, and impossible to truly explain. I highly recommend that you embark upon your own journey with the medicine.

Who is serving Ayahuasca and how are they qualified?

My intention is to steer every reader in the direction that is aligned with the sacred practices of the medicine ayahuasca.

When looking to sit with this medicine, it is important to sit with a healer who has had the long-term training with Indigenous lineages that have been practicing ayahuasca.

Why is it important to sit with Indigenous lineages or folks heavily trained by Indigenous lineages ?

The Indigenous lineages like the Ashaninka people of Peru in the Mayantuyacu lineage of Maestro Juan Flores Salazar have been sitting with the medicine's ways and practicing for hundreds if not thousands of years. They've learned how to navigate the medicine and have learned the nuances of serving the medicine well.

When we come from a culture that just doesn't know what they don't know, it becomes crucial to sit with folks who have practiced with the Indigenous lineage that provides the long-term training needed to hold a safe space for participants to have a safe journey.

To find practitioners who are rooted in a lineage and who have been practicing for a long time ask, "In what ways are they in relationship with the lineage and the ones who practiced?" A key factor expressed by Mayantuyacu lineage is how important it is to be in relationship and reciprocity to the ones who have carried the medicine forward in time.

Aya is not psychological work or biomedical work, the work is energetic and shamanic. In order to work with this medicine, the development of energetic and shamanic awareness, skills, and tools, for all cultures is a very long process. It usually takes years and decades, and involves sitting with the medicine hundreds or even thousands of times. The path for an ayahuasquero or ayahuasquera is not an easy path but a long, developmental one. The ayahuasquero spends months undergoing long plant dietas, learning the sacred geometric design of the plants, healing within, and instilling deeper wisdom and healing in order to carry the medicine with the integrity, the support, and the plant allies needed for ceremonial practice so that the healer can ultimately hold a safe and clear space for participants no matter what comes up for them in the mental, physical, and/or spiritual realms. It is a long process.

When deciding who to sit with, aim for someone who has undergone the long training needed from an Indigenous lineage. Always ask for references, always make sure you trust who is serving, and always know the experience and training the person has had.

Aya Preparation

The preparation for Aya is key to being able to receive the medicine in the most harmonious way. Before sitting with Aya, I was vegan for six years and found that the way the medicine moved through my body was very peaceful.

I always take the preparation very intentionally and seriously. I see this as the time to create the most fertile soil in my body so that Aya can go in, go deep, and get to the gold nuggets as best as possible. Gold nuggets meaning the bigger lessons needed to powerfully transform a habitual pattern that is limiting or keeps one stuck in the same cycle.

How do we create fertile soil in the body?

I have found eating organically plant-based, going fully vegan, and eating only whole foods leads to the most successful experience. I eliminate all foods that come in wrappers and that are not in their natural state three weeks prior to a ceremony. In the mornings, I indulge in a blend of oats, buckwheat, and amaranth with no sugar added. In the afternoon and evenings, I flow with lentils and quinoa to get my complete amino acid profile for protein. I add broccoli, microgreens, and avocado with Himalayan sea salt. Throughout the day, I snack on sprouted walnuts, pecans, pine nuts, and almonds. I intake mostly water with the occasional coconut water (from the actual coconut) and organic teas. I eliminate all caffeine and processed drinks as well.

Two weeks before I sit with Aya, I sit with the Kambo medicine for two days back to back, setting the intention that I want to anchor in with Aya. I see this as doing the deep cleaning before Abuela comes to town. Sitting with Kambo beforehand has allowed for the focus of the medicine to go into the spiritual, conscious, energetic body instead of spending most of the time cleaning the physical body.

What is Kambo?

Kambo, aslo known as the Amazonian monkey frog, is a day time medicine that is very physical, a non-psychedelic experience, and short-lasting. Kambo is a frog secretion containing many bio-peptides and is reported to be one of the strongest natural antibiotics and anesthetics, and one of the strongest, natural ways to boost our immune system, clear chronic Fatigue Syndrome, chronic pain, cancer, HIV, HPV, herpes, Parkinson's disease, multiple sclerosis , Alzheimer's, depression, blood pressure issues, thyroid issues, hepatitis, diabetes, rheumatism, Lyme disease, arthritis, addictions, emotional trauma and many more.

Kambo has a detoxifying effect on the internal organs, including the liver, the intestines, as well as the entire digestive system. Many tribes also use Kambo as the antidote for snake bites, as a medicine for many illnesses, and as an overall health tonic.

Kambo is commonly known as the "Great Revealer." Properly administered ceremonies focus on bringing forth personal strength and empowerment, while focusing our intentions on creating a stronger body, mind, and spirit. In the jungle, the tribes utilize this medicine before a hunt because they would move and process faster and more efficiently post- Kambo.

This is a very physical experience. For twenty minutes, the participant has to endure acute nausea, with relief coming from purgative releases. A true power boost to your immune system, and physical cleanse like no other. The ensuing mental clarity and energy are a massive payoff, however.

After Kambo, I eliminate all sugars and go deeper in my meditation practice. The process starts with an hour of meditation in the morning, thirty minutes in the middle of the day if possible, and another hour at night right before I go to sleep. Before each meditation, I journal on the intention of loving my healthy body and receiving Aya with love, and being open, creating intentional space for her to come in and feel welcomed.

Through this process, when it is time to sit with the medicine, I feel as though I prepared the best environment for her, to optimize receiving the healing. Once I have sat with the medicine, post-ceremony I continue the same practices for two to four more weeks, eating super cleanly, meditating, and journaling every day. This allows for the medicine to have a healthy, safe container to continue to do its healing work. Every three months, at the change of the season, I start the process again of welcoming and connecting with the essence of Mother Earth and all she has to teach.

I have found great success in this process. It is as though every season I am able to see life with new perspective, new clarity, and new insight while healing my body in deeper ways. This process has demonstrated the power of "doing the work" to heal within and the magnificent positive shifts that come with the sacrifice of devotion.

JMG Poetry Introduction

"We teach from the radiance of our own discovery."
– Tara Brach

Welcome. My name is Jackie Guerra, and through these pages, I invite you into my journey of transformation and healing. This book is more than just a collection of stories; it's an offering of my own discoveries, a path that led me from confusion and disconnection to alignment and love. If you stay with me, you'll witness the profound ways that the power of plants, the wisdom of ancient ceremonies, and the sacred act of listening to our own bodies can change a life.

Throughout these pages, we will explore the nature of healing— what it means to come home to oneself. Central themes include the power of plant medicine, the importance of self-awareness, and the profound healing that happens when we reconnect to our authentic selves. You'll see how societal pressures, unresolved childhood trauma, and the modern world's pace kept me in a constant state of disconnection, and how through plant medicine, I found a way to heal the wounds of the past. This is a story of liberation, from conforming to roles that didn't fit, to uncovering my true nature, and the profound realization that every part of us—body, mind, and spirit—must be in harmony to reach our highest potential.

I grew up a tomboy in Plano, Texas, navigating a world that seemed determined to tell me who I should be. As a first-generation Puerto Rican-American, I straddled cultures and expectations, excelling in sports while wrestling with my identity. It wasn't until high school, when I spent a transformative summer in California, that I first understood my romantic feelings for a close friend; the realization that I could love a girl changed everything. But societal pressures, rumors, and rejection made me hide my truth, while simultaneously pushing me toward my soccer dreams, eventually earning a scholarship to the University of Illinois.

College brought its own set of challenges. I was diagnosed with ADHD, and under the influence of medications, I struggled to sit still and fit in academically. But it was my passion for soccer, and the desire to push past limits, that led me to develop my own fitness program, transforming myself into one of the fittest players on the team. This experience showed me that resilience and inner strength were key to overcoming adversity. Still, something inside me remained unsettled, and I continued searching for deeper meaning.

It wasn't until I moved to Los Angeles that the universe began to reveal its wisdom. Living by the ocean, diving into alternative healing practices, and experimenting with plant-based diets and reiki, I began to see how my body and mind could align with the rhythms of nature. This alignment brought clarity and healing, but it wasn't until I met plant medicine—ayahuasca—that the deepest parts of my soul began to surface. The medicine taught me to sit with my pain, to uncover trauma I had long buried, and to love the parts of myself that had been hidden for so long.

My hope is that this book becomes a mirror, a companion for those walking their own healing journey. The intention is to shine a light on the sacred practices that have allowed me to rediscover myself and to inspire you to explore these paths for yourself. There is so much wisdom within the Earth, within the plants, and within each of us. I believe that by aligning our mind, body, and spirit, we can manifest our highest potential, transforming pain into purpose, and trauma into liberation.

So, I invite you to come with me. Let's heal. Let's step into the fullness of who we are, and in doing so, ripple that healing into the world.

Wisdom From Ayahuasca

Wisdom of Fruit

Roots are the anchor of the tree
The force to withstand life with ease
Wind is the movement that awakens the dance
Water is the nourishment that brings strength to the stance
Sun is the life force that allows for growth
Devotion is the thread that brings fruit to oath

Sabiduría de Fruta

Las raíces de la planta la anclan a la tierra.
La fuerza para soportar la vida con facilidad.
El viento es el movimiento que despierta la danza.
El agua es el alimento que aporta firmeza a la postura.
El sol es la fuente vital que permite el crecimiento.
La devoción es el hilo que da fruto al juramento.

Wisdom of Strength

Wisdom of strength
Defiance of remembrance
The art of life tree
Is grounding in conscious clarity

Physical movement
Brings integration to soul development
Strong temple
Takes
time
to assemble

Intention of peace
Letting go of attachment with ease
Muscles are the contractions
Of soul to physical interactions

Sabiduría de Fuerza

Sabiduría de la fuerza,
desafío al recuerdo.
El arte del árbol
está fundamentado en la claridad consciente.

El movimiento físico
aporta integración
al desarrollo del alma.
Templo fuerte.
Toma
tiempo
para ensamblar.

Intención de paz.
Dejar ir el apego con facilidad,
los músculos son las contracciones
del alma a las interacciones físicas.

Wisdom of Beauty

Wisdom of beauty
Is living in pure authenticity

Staying clear of all blockages and thought forms that bring distraction
So that mind doesn't project distortions

Seizing the unique geometric design
Allows for physical form to align

Sabiduría de Belleza

Sabiduría de belleza
es vivir desde la autenticidad.

Mantenerse alejado de los pensamientos que bloquean y distraen,
para que la mente no proyecte distorsión.

Recibiendo diseño geométrico
se alinea el cuerpo físico.

Wisdom of Intelligence

Wisdom of intelligence
Lives in diligence

Creative outlook to perceive new subject
Openness allows for the initiation of project

Guidance and focus bring life to object
Object shifts to objective

Levels unwind in specific progression
Soul observes as mind experiences digestion

Of new information that ignites curiosity
New mental pathways unlocked vicariously...

Sabiduría de Inteligencia

Sabiduría de inteligencia
vive en diligencia.

Creatividad para ver desde la subjetividad,
abre iniciación a un nuevo proyecto.

Enfoque y persistencia traen vida.
La vida mueve al objeto.

Niveles que se desarrollan,
el espíritu observa mientras la mente recibe.

Nueva información que enciende la curiosidad,
puertas que se abren indirectamente.
Vive en diligencia.

Creatividad para ver desde la subjetividad,
abre iniciación a un nuevo proyecto.

Enfoque y persistencia traen vida,
la vida mueve al objeto.

Niveles que se desarrollan,
el espíritu observa mientras la mente recibe.

Nueva información que enciende la curiosidad,
puertas que se abren indirectamente.

Wisdom of Health

Wisdom of health
Is exponential wealth

Divine ability to see value of body
Our cells' ability to flow infinitely

Creating decisions, thought patterns aligned with Earth frequency
So that our photons are fueled by Sun's energy

Vitaly blossoms and zest for life grows
The more we put organic plants in, the body knows

Exactly how to function
Aligned consumption

Intentional eating
Leads to healthy heart beating

Sabiduría de Salud

Sabiduría de salud
es riqueza de verdad.

Habilidad divina de ver el valor del cuerpo
y cómo las células se mueven por dentro.

Creando decisiones que se alinean con la frecuencia de la Madre
Tierra
para que los fotones sean impulsados por el sol.

Vitalidad nace y alegría crece
cuando consumimos plantas.
El cuerpo reconoce lo orgánico.

Exactamente cómo funciona
un cuerpo alineado.

Comiendo intencionalmente
se manifiesta un corazón fuerte.

Wisdom of Peace

Wisdom of peace
Is living life with ease

Desire to see without perception
Gives space for open interpretation

Diversity is the essence of life
Not everyone is a husband or a wife

Quantum uniqueness is the fabric of natural expansiveness
Conscious awareness of the thread of oneness

Ability to see with compassion
Leads to soul, mind, and body satisfaction

Differences in color, gender, religion, ethnicity
Is like loving bird, butterfly, dragonfly, and bee

All here for their unique ability
We all hold the power to see

Sabiduría de Paz

Sabiduría de paz
estoy viviendo con los demás.

Poder ver sin percepción,
da espacio para la interpretación.

Diversidad es la esencia de la vida.
No todas las personas se casan ni son mamá o papá.

Unicidad cuántica es el tejido de la expansividad,
presencia consciente del hilo de la unidad.

La capacidad de ver con compasión
conduce a la satisfacción del alma, la mente y el cuerpo.

Diferencia en color, sexo y origen étnico.
Se ama igual a la mariposa, a la libélula, a la abeja o al pájaro.

Todos con su habilidad única,
todos tenemos el poder de verlo todo.

Wisdom of Love

Wisdom of love
Is flying soaring above

Perceptions of control
Letting go of the need to play a role

Freedom of choice
Freedom to rejoice

In the art of allowing
So appreciation keeps flowing

Extinction of jealousy
Eradication of fallacy

Entering process with diplomacy
So all parties feel harmony

Sabiduría del Amor

Sabiduría del amor,
es volar arriba del temor.

La percepción del control,
dejar la necesidad de jugar en una posición.

Libertad de decisión,
libertad de alegrarse.

Es el arte de dar sustancia
la erradicación de la falacia.

Entrando en proceso con diplomacia,
para que todas las partes sientan armonía.

Wisdom of Sun

Heat, fire, energetic life force
Frequency that transmits heat like strong horse

The ingredient that allows for all beings to come alive
The one component that allows for plants to thrive

Ingenuity, light intelligence
Warmth of sun gives remembrance

Of vitality
Instinctual cosmic reality

Source of life that brings fruit to the stem
Vibrant, capitulating beam, the emblem

The philosophical master creator
Silent, loud in it's high elevator

Destroyer and grower
The one who blossoms the flower

Ripens the fruit
Expanding conscious pursuit

Sabiduría del Sol

Calor, fuego, energía de vida y valor.
Frecuencia que transmite color.

El ingrediente que da luz a cada vida,
el componente que le permite crecer a la planta.

Inteligencia e ingenio.
El calor del sol invoca al recuerdo.

Fuente de vida que trae fruto al tallo.
Haz vibrante y capitular, el emblema.

El maestro creador filosófico.
Silencioso, ruidoso y ascensor.

Destructor y cultivador.
La que florece es la flor.

Madura la fruta
ampliando la búsqueda de la consciencia.

Wisdom of the Moon

Wisdom of moon
Divine Spirit that unveils monsoon

The mover of wobble on axis, creating stable climate
Force creating tidal breaking habit

White light in dark night
Shimmering down energies of insight

Waxing and waning
Continuously changing

Cyclical multidimensional teachings
When to plant, when to prune, when to start bleeding

Emotional elicitor of heart transcending
Muse for mirror work and manifesting

Charger of crystals in the fullness of cycle
Restoring and teaching when to recycle

Divine teacher, priestess of the mysteries of alchemy
Paradox revealer to bridge time space functionality

Sabiduría de Luna

Sabiduría de Luna,
espíritu divino que trae la tormenta.

El motor de la oscilación actúa sobre el eje creando un clima estable,
fuerza que crea el hábito de romper las olas.

Luz blanca en cielo negro,
resplandecientes energías del conocimiento.

La luna crece y decrece constantemente.

Enseñanzas cíclicas multidimensionales.
¿Cuándo plantar, cuándo podar, cuándo empezar a sangrar?

Musa que trabajar con espejos al manifestarse,
elicitor emocional de corazón trascendiente.

Divina Maestra, sacerdotisa de alquimia y misterio.
Revelador de paradojas al unir la funcionalidad del espacio-tiempo.

Wisdom of Ocean

The overflowing rhythm of the ocean
Infinite waters, healing potion

Ecosystem that inhabits
Divine animals with divine spirits

Salt to cleanse all wounds
Tides that move with the changing of moon

Healing crystalline liquid glass
Habitat that needs our protection to grasp

The importance of phytoplankton
To the majestic whales to the exoskeleton

Quantum intelligence in each inhabitant
Coral reefs, Mother Earth's brain, to shark strength, so vigilant

Fishies of all sizes, lengths, and colors,
Each creating a web of vectors

All beings divinely placed like essential keys
Mother Earth's sanctuary

Sabiduría de Océano

El ritmo desbordante del océano,
aguas infinitas que todo lo curan.

Ecosistema que habita
animales divinos con espíritus mágicos.

Sal que limpia todas las heridas,
mareas que se mueven con las fases de la luna.

Vidrio líquido, cristalino y curativo.
Hábitat que necesita nuestra protección para prevalecer.

La importancia del phytoplankton,
a las majestuosas ballenas en su exoesqueleto.

Inteligencia cuántica en cada habitante,
fuerza de tiburón tan vigilante.

Peces de todos los tamaños y colores,
cada uno creando una red de vectores.

Todos los seres divinamente colocados,
llaves esenciales al santuario de la Madre Tierra.

Wisdom of Faith

Wisdom of faith
Is ability to bathe

In the sincere desire to illuminate
Darkness, challenge, struggle that accumulate

Integrity in the thought process to believe
In one's desires to achieve

Throwing anchor down to uphold
The vision of what one desires to mold

Sabíduria de Fe

Sabiduría de fe,
es la capacidad para curarse.

El sincero deseo de iluminar la oscuridad,
desafíos y luchas que se acumulan.

Integridad en el proceso de pensamiento,
en el deseo de lograrlo.

Echando anclas para sostener
la visión de lo que se desea transformar.

Wisdom of Relationship

Wisdom of relationship
Knowing each is on ship
Mirrors of moments to heal
When experiences erupt to reveal

Anger, frustration, or rejection
Moments that lead to self-realization
Reflection of self in each interaction
Choosing to heal inside strengthens clarity instead of projection

Bond strengthens when both see
The mirror of awareness is fluidity
To flow instead of resist
Being patient is the ingredient over insist

Hands held strong, kiss felt deep
When two souls know the power of free instead of keep
Letting the pieces fall as they may
Giving space to let the other say

Expressing with gentle notion
Letting heart feel emotion
To awaken sense of self and solution
Relationship is the process of clearing illusion

Sabiduría de Relaciones

Sabiduría de relaciones,
entendiendo que somos conexiones.
Espejo para sanar, no para ganar.

Frustración o rechazo que crea tensión,
momentos que conducen a la autorrealización,
reflejo de uno mismo en cada interacción.
Elegir sanar por dentro fortalece la claridad en lugar de la proyección.

El vínculo se fortalece cuando ambos ven,
el espejo de la conciencia es la fluidez.
Fluir en lugar de resistir,
ser paciente es el ingrediente para no insistir.

Manos apretadas con fuerza y un beso profundo.
Cuando dos almas conocen el poder de liberarse y no de conservarse,
dejando caer las piezas sin caretas,
dar espacio para que el otro exista a su manera.

Expresando con gentil noción,
dejando que el corazón siente emoción,
despertar el sentido de uno mismo y de la solución,
la relación es el proceso de limpiar la ilusión.

Wisdom of Mountain

Wisdom of Mountain
Is the metaphor of the fountain

Skyscrapers of rock, granite
Symbolic translation of the infinite

Wisdom embodied in each crack and crevice
To show spirit how to be of service

How to climb in fatigue, fear, or doubt
To bring new strength like sprout

Master of standing tall
Demonstrating no such thing as wall

Sabiduría de Montaña

Sabiduría de montaña
es la metáfora de la fuente.

Rascacielos de roca y granito,
traducción simbólica del infinito.

Sabiduría encarnada en cada grieta
para mostrarle al espíritu cómo ser útil.

Wisdom embodied in each crack
to show spirit how to be of service.

Escalar en la fatiga, el miedo o la duda,
inhalar nueva fuerza como un brote.

Maestro empinado de alturas infinitas,
demostrando que no hay muros en una consciencia clara.

CHAPTER 1
WINTER: DARKNESS

I
Winter: DARKNESS

Opening the doors so gently
Movement is driven by source energy

Breathing deeper into the essence of light
Aya brings thee down into the darkest of night

Sweet medicine of the soul
Time to purify to become whole.

Movement felt cellularly
Distinct shifts internally

The flickering of light starts to shimmer
Into the depths of darkness where the light was never

Tears of gratitude as I feel her hold me tight
From there, the fire of her clearing ignites

Intra-cellular molecular DNA undoing
Waves of heat and nausea emerging

Examples of selection-making
Patterns of consciousness not meant to keep creating

Discomfort with the wrong choices of the past
I sit still, acknowledging, freeing thy heart at last

Piercing through thick blockages of old decisions misaligned with
heart intention
I stay calm and give it attention

Forgiveness rather than detention
Freedom instead of tension

Somatic expression of suspension
Heart beating fast, a new dimension

Calling in grace, to unlace and apologize
Sorry to those I affected and to myself whom I demonized

Light into all aspects of the karmic past I never realized
Moments of the past expressed and visualized

Like rain coming down hard to remove a shield
Calmness, looking into the eyes of what needs to be healed

Deep precipice of guilt and shame
Humility transforms the blame

Clearing voices rooted in negative gain
Undoing throat, creating a new lane

Movement, the winds of eternal vacuum
Removing all the remanence and gloom

Darkness and light of Aya's kingdom
Transformed to heart freedom

Ceremony ending
So much more to continue exploring...

Abriendo las puertas suavemente,
creando espacio para que la medicina ingrese.

Movimiento guiado por la Madre
que se siente en la sangre.

Entrando a espacios muy oscuros,
a los que yo nunca he ido.

La inteligencia de Aya guiando,
y yo me quedo mirando.

Nuevos pensamientos entran:
"Quiero sanar todos los momentos
en los que inconscientemente lastimé a alguien".

Memorias de repente,
pido perdón con la mente.

Memorias de repente,
pido perdón con el corazón.

Una gran oración.

Aya entra profundamente
aclarando las energías
que le impiden a la luz llegar a la mente.

Creando espacio,
un río hirviendo.

Aclarando colores,
limpiando voces.

Humildad plantada en cada célula,
le doy gracias a las lecciones que la vida me enseña.

Momentos expresados y visualizados,
luz en todos los espacios del pasado kármico.

Mirando a los ojos de todo aquello que necesita ser sanado,
al igual que la lluvia cae con fuerza para quitarse el escudo.

Profundo precipicio de culpa y vergüenza,
la humildad transforma la secuencia.

Movimiento, los vientos del vacío eterno
quitando la tristeza de mi cuerpo.

La oscuridad
enseña la verdad.

Final de la ceremonia,
corazón agradecido.

La medicina aclara todo,
hay más para seguir explorando.

Un nuevo espejo
sigo mirando.

Layers / Capas

Rocking gently into Aya's loving embrace
Transcending darkness into cellular grace

Softly moving through with cosmic strength
Stretching so wide, giving elegance in length

Humble, movement so tender
Weaving brings union to gender

Left   Right
Masculine   Feminine

All one within

Snakes emerge, I accept with love
Insects show up, I become white dove

Sharks flowing in, I receive with a hug
Lion roars, I let go of the judge

Predators, masters of light
The union of all, shines bright

Shadow so uncovered like roots in the ground
Acknowledged, we are now bound

Humility
I am the strand of hair on mother's belly
One of many

Little speck here I stand
I am a grain of sand
Left and right are now holding hands

The opening of heart unlocked by "sorry"
Lack of attention to shadow energy

Turns out to be essential to the story
Darkness is the light connected to glory

Meciéndome, sintiendo su abrazo,
cada respiración, un beso...

La frecuencia de ayahuasca.
La energia de mamá.

En la oscuridad
la humildad más profunda.

Serpientes, insectos,
movimientos.

Tiburón, león...
Aya enseña la unión.

Todo es parte de la creación,
el tambor y la guitarra en una canción.

Juntos sin tener que ser enemigos:
Izquierda   Femenina
Derecho   Masculino

Familia por dentro,
somos uno.

Realización de que la sombra es parte de mí,
creando las lecciones que aprendí.

De la consciencia Divina,
experiencia de Pachamama.

El invierno es para destapar,
nutrir y dejar.

Allí abren las puertas de corazón,
entendiendo que todo es una oración.

Álbumes maravillosas,
cada tema precisamente puesto.

Notas bajas, notas altas,
pausas.

La vida es la ceremonia.
Consciencia la directora.

Union / Unión

II
Winter: REALIZATIONS

Patience is

Silence

For unknown amounts of moments
Ingredients are components

Segmenting allows for understanding
Like water absorbing

Soil freezing
Roots growing

Leaves dying
Life is shedding

La paciencia es:

Silencio.

En cantidades desconocidas,
los ingredientes son los componentes.

Segmentar, permite
entender cómo absorber el agua.

Congelación del suelo,
raíces creciendo.

Hojas muriendo,
la vida derramando.

Duality / Dualidad

Cold, darkness
Stars talking as mistress

Moonlight
White light

Skin absorbing in delight
Bird is taking flight

Darkness, thy friend
To heal all old wounds to transcend

Pain into freedom
Walls to kingdom

Screams into singing
Trauma into learning

Basking in moonlight
Full and so bright

Emerging feelings
Are lightning when it's striking

Transcendence of diminishing power
Letting go of the past that no longer matters

Healed, sad to happier
As moon enlightens dark matter

Shadow thy friend
We sit together again and again

Learning lessons of my suffering
To alchemize the sterling into gold shining

Unlocking doors
To places never been before...

Disfrutando de la luz de la luna,
yendo a la oscuridad más profunda.

Compartiendo con la sombra,
conversación para entender a la compositora.

Para sanar las viejas heridas, para trascender
como la oscuridad se convierte en claridad para ver.

Descubriendo los misterios del sufrimiento,
alquimizar la libra esterlina hasta convertirla en oro.

Dolor en libertad,
mentiras a la verdad.

Muros en el reino,
caos a la paz por dentro.

Abriendo las puertas de la consciencia negra.
Todo es parte de la tierra.

Healing light / Luz sanadora

III
Winter: INTEGRATION

Master Interpreter
Shadows appear
To show us how to see clear

Master Interpreter
Giving us a choice
To use our voice

Master Interpreter
Self realization
Rooted in purification

Master Interpreter
Knowing that the contrast is serving its purpose
That the opposite is the creator of the opposite

Master Interpreter
The solution is the effort driven to understand optimal perspectives
In order to hold the "right" objectives

Master Interpreter
Realizing there is no right or left
Just turns and overall directions
Being one with internal indications

Master Interpreter
No right or wrong way
Just journeying along each day
Learning to be an independent observer
United thinker

Master interpreter

Maestra intérprete,
sombras aparecen
para enseñarnos cómo ver.

Maestra intérprete,
danos una opción
para ver la solución.

Maestra intérprete,
autorrealización,
arraigada a la purificación.

Maestra intérprete,
saber que el contraste cumple con su propósito,
que lo contrario es creador de lo contrario.

Maestra intérprete,
la solución es el esfuerzo realizado para comprender
las perspectivas óptimas.
Tomar medidas en los objetivos "correctos".

Maestra intérprete,
sabiendo que no hay derecha ni izquierda,
solo giros y direcciones generales.
Ser uno con indicaciones internas.

Maestra intérprete,
no hay manera correcta o incorrecta,
simplemente viajando cada día,
aprendiendo a ser una observadora independiente.
Unida pensadora,

Maestra intérprete.

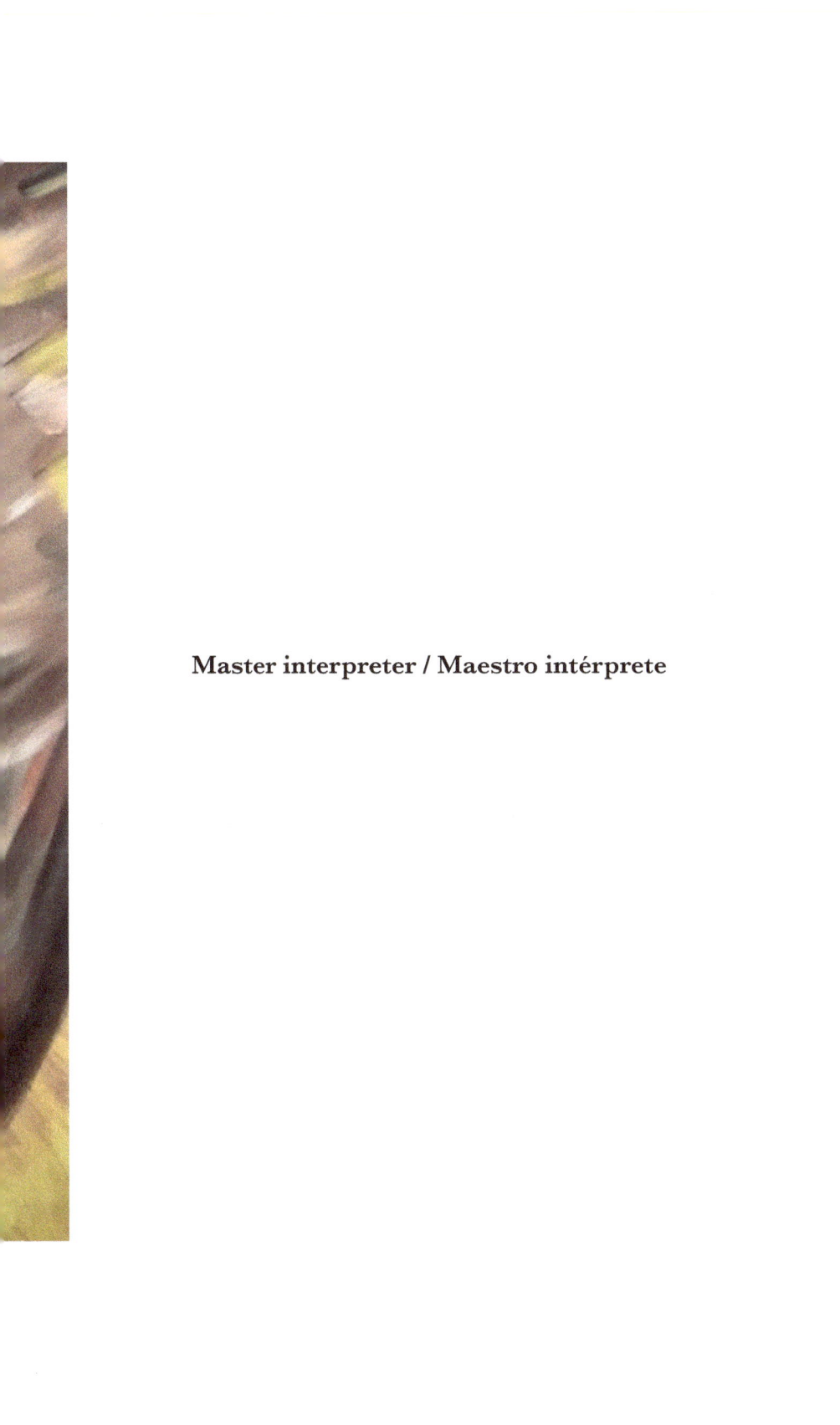

Master interpreter / Maestro intérprete

IV
Winter : PRAYER

I trust
I let go of lust
Nothing stays the same
I let go of shame

Everything is subject to change
I create the direction I chose to engage
Whether I like it or not
I must let go of trying to create a knot
I surrender, I let it flow
Into where it's supposed to go

I am letting go of pain
I am letting fears fall like rain
To purify heart, mind, body, and soul
Clearing to make spaces for a new bowl

To be received
To be shared
To be given

The recycling of all things is a given
I follow the patterns of Earth's highest quest
Knowing she wants us to just try our best

To detach
Hatch
Let go

Breathe in and let the air flow
The wisdom pouring in so I get to grow
The value of what we live is written in
The moments of self-realization within

Letting go of external validation and collection
I am clearing space for heart
Soul recollection

Estoy dejando ir el dolor
y los miedos para purificar
mi corazón, mente, alma y cuerpo.

Limpiar para hacer espacio,
un nuevo vaso.

Beber de un nuevo amor y reponerme.
Reciclar es parte de crecer.

Sigo los patrones de la búsqueda más alta de la tierra,
sabiendo que ella quiere que hagamos nuestro mejor esfuerzo.

Escotilla.
Dejarlo ir.

Respiro y dejo que el aire fluya,
la sabiduría fluyendo para que pueda crecer.
Valor en lo que vivimos,
momentos de autorrealización.

Dejar de lado la validación y recopilación externas.
Estoy limpiando espacio para el corazón,
recuperándome del alma y la razón.

CHAPTER 2
SPRING: TRANSFORMATION

I.
Spring: POEMS OF CEREMONY

Thawing
Feeling warmth entering

Sweet silky smooth
Flowing through thy veins nude

Initiating gentle energetic cellular release
Starting with my hands and arms with ease

Like gentle mudslides clearing space
Ayawhauska moving through all crevices to unlace

Layers of energetic memories within each muscle
Releasing hands, arms, shoulders, old hustle

Moving through neck, spine, chest, and back
Shedding all old bark, thought forms of lack

Slithering down to hips
Opening the legs like mouth opening lips

Disintegrating memories of hands unwanted
Cellular remembrance of childhood haunted

Placing my hands, a wand of light
To slay away the past with Aya's insight

Thighs to knees
Unraveling Aya sees

It's time to reset my legs
No longer pegs

Transformation of stretching
Lengthening

Emerging pain
Breaking through reins

Scolding from teachers
Being taken out of the game, sitting on bleachers

Aya moves to the feet, ankles, calves
Carving out the weights, anchors of the past

Light beams flow into never-before-seen open space
The essence of new life awakens to take place

The years of physical defeat
Cleared with Aya's heat

The power that the "I am" is so true
Sprouting into new...

Dulce, suave y sedosa,
fluyendo por mis venas desnuda.

Inicia una suave liberación celular energética,
comenzando con facilidad en mis manos y brazos.

Igual que suaves deslizamientos de tierra que limpian el espacio,
moviéndose a través de todas las grietas por desatar.

Capas de recuerdos energéticos dentro de cada músculo.
Soltando manos, brazos, hombros... un viejo ajetreo.

Moviéndose por el cuello, la columna, el pecho y la espalda.
Derramando toda la corteza añeja.

Deslizándose hasta las caderas,
abriendo las piernas como la boca lo hace con los labios.

Colocando mis manos,
varita de luz para terminar con las experiencias pasadas
y la perspectiva de Aya.

Es hora de restablecer las piernas, ya no son clavijas.
Transformación de estiramiento y alargamiento.

Dolor emergente,
rompiendo cuidadosamente las viejas cadenas.

Pasando a florecer en frecuencias sinérgicas,
recibiendo la recompensa.

Aya se mueve hacia las pantorrillas, los tobillos y las piernas.
Tallando los pesos, anclas viejas.

Los rayos de luz fluyen hacia un nuevo espacio abierto,
la esencia de una nueva vida es una puerta que se abre con el viento.

El poder del "yo soy" es tan cierto.
Brotando hacia lo nuevo...

Sprouting / Abriéndonos

Seed has blueprint
I sit in amazement

The web of truth uncovering the web of lies
I lay and surrender
I fly
High
Stillness
Pure bliss

Uncovering and healing

From the highest,
the steepest,
the deepest,

All at once
Coming undone

To be put back together
Much better

La semilla tiene un plano,
me siento asombrado.

La red de la verdad descubre la red de las mentiras,
me acuesto y me entrego,
vuelo alto,
quietud,
pura felicidad.

Descubriendo y sanando

desde lo más alto,
lo más empinado,
lo más profundo.

Todo a la vez,
deshaciéndose,
para volver a armarse,
mucho mejor.

Undoing / Deshaciendo

Wake up pretty eyes that were once weary
You see now more clearly

Connect with the frequency of Mother Earth
Great friend, energy of rebirth

Divine protector, ally
You feel thee inside

You are aligned, pure sacred
Protected from all energies of hatred

Be confident

While running
Dancing
Playing
Singing

Agua Florida flows in
I sit in deep appreciation

For this beautiful experience
Aya's divine intelligence

Energy so powerful
So beautiful

I am you, we are we
Aya inside forever in perfect harmony

Despierta, ojitos lindos,
que ahora ven más claro.

Conecta con la frecuencia de La Madre Tierra.
Mejor amiga,
divina protectora...
La sientes por dentro.

Estás alineada, pura, sagrada.
En su energía ten confianza.

A caminar.
A correr.
A bailar.
A cantar.
A jugar.
A vivir.

Ya sabes quién soy,
para arriba yo voy.

La energía divina femenina.
La energía divino femenino.
Ya lo sé,
soy una con ambas.

Cada palabra, cada acción,
con Gaia's dirección.

Protegida.
Le doy gracias a la vida
por esta experiencia tan linda.
¡Qué linda es la energía que rescata la vida!

Movimiento por dentro,
altura con precipicio.

Energía tan poderosa,
tan bella,
tan inteligente.
moviéndose como una serpiente.

Con calma, respira.
Ella es mia, yo soy Aya,
juntas llenas de lágrimas.
por la conexión de mi corazón.

Put back together / Recomponer

The movement inside
Letting it reside
Union / uncovering / like an onion

So / many / layers
Quantum time space healing

Surrendering
Feeling cells heating

Thy heart beating
Gentle inside
Mother Earth guide

She takes me with her
Burning all my scars
Disintegrating bars

I grow deeper in surrender,
She calls me under
No struggle
No fight
This is part of thy light

Still
Rolling downhill
Staying calm
The mind has many alarms
No need for firearms
Time to clear
Allowing Aya to steer

The fears inside arise
No need to hide
Fear excretes
Heart heats

She sees
With a loving eye
Loving embrace
She eats it with her grace

Feeling my deepest fears
Transforming to my biggest strength
Alchemy of Earth spirit
Power to move through it

Awakening
Divine timing
She brought me down
Healed thy frown

Beautiful unity with pain, suffering
Somatic healing
Soil is fertile to begin growing....

El movimiento interior,
dejándolo residir.

Unión / descubriendo / como una cebolla / tantas / capas.
Sanación cuántica del tiempo y el espacio

Entregándose,
sintiendo el calor de las células.

Tu corazón suave latiendo por dentro,
guía de la Madre Tierra que me lleva con ella.

Quemando todas mis cicatrices,
desintegrando los barrotes.

Crezco profundamente en la rendición,
ella me llama.

Sin lucha, sin pelea,
es parte de la luz.

Aún así, rodando cuesta abajo
manteniendo la calma.

La mente tiene muchas alarmas,
no hay necesidad de armas de fuego.

Tiempo para aclararlo todo,
permitiendo que Aya sea guía.

Los miedos surgen en mi interior,
no hay necesidad de esconderse.

El miedo se excreta,
el corazón se calienta.

Ella ve con ojos lindos y un abrazo amoroso.
Ella lo come con su gracia.

Sintiendo mis miedos más profundos,
transformándome en mi mayor fortaleza,
alquimia del espíritu de la tierra.
Poder para atravesarlo.

Despertar.
Tiempo divino.
Ella me derribó.
Sanó tu ceño.

Hermosa unidad con el dolor y el sufrimiento,
sanación somática.
El suelo es fértil para comenzar a crecer.

Fertile soil / Suelo fértil

II.
Spring: REALIZATIONS

In this beautiful blue
Underneath light hue

Seeing and experiencing
Releasing the old to bring in the new

Shedding bark
Is light entering dark

A new chapter officially starts...

En este hermoso azul,
debajo del tono claro.

Viendo y experimentando,
liberar lo viejo para traer lo nuevo.

Igual a la corteza que se derrama,
la luz entra a la oscuridad.

Oficialmente un nuevo capítulo inicia.

New chapter / Nuevo capítulo

Breathe deep
Feel the energy beneath
Waves of air corresponding
Bridging
Surging
The ocean floors
Heart beat roars
Unwavering truth, igniting youth!

Reality

Destiny of flying up, above, and below thoughts of immortality

I am consciously transcending
Undoing yet receiving
Releasing while absorbing
Disintegrating while growing

Opening up to be
            the butterfly
                        of eternity

Respira profundo,
siente la energía moviéndose,
surgiendo desde el fondo del océano.
El latido del corazón ruge
encendiendo la juventud.

Verdad.
Inquebrantable.
Realidad.

El destino es volar arriba y abajo de la profundidad.
Estoy trascendiendo conscientemente.

Deshacer y aún recibir,
liberar mientras absorbo,
desintegrar mientras crezco,
abriéndome para ser:

La mariposa

de la eternidad.

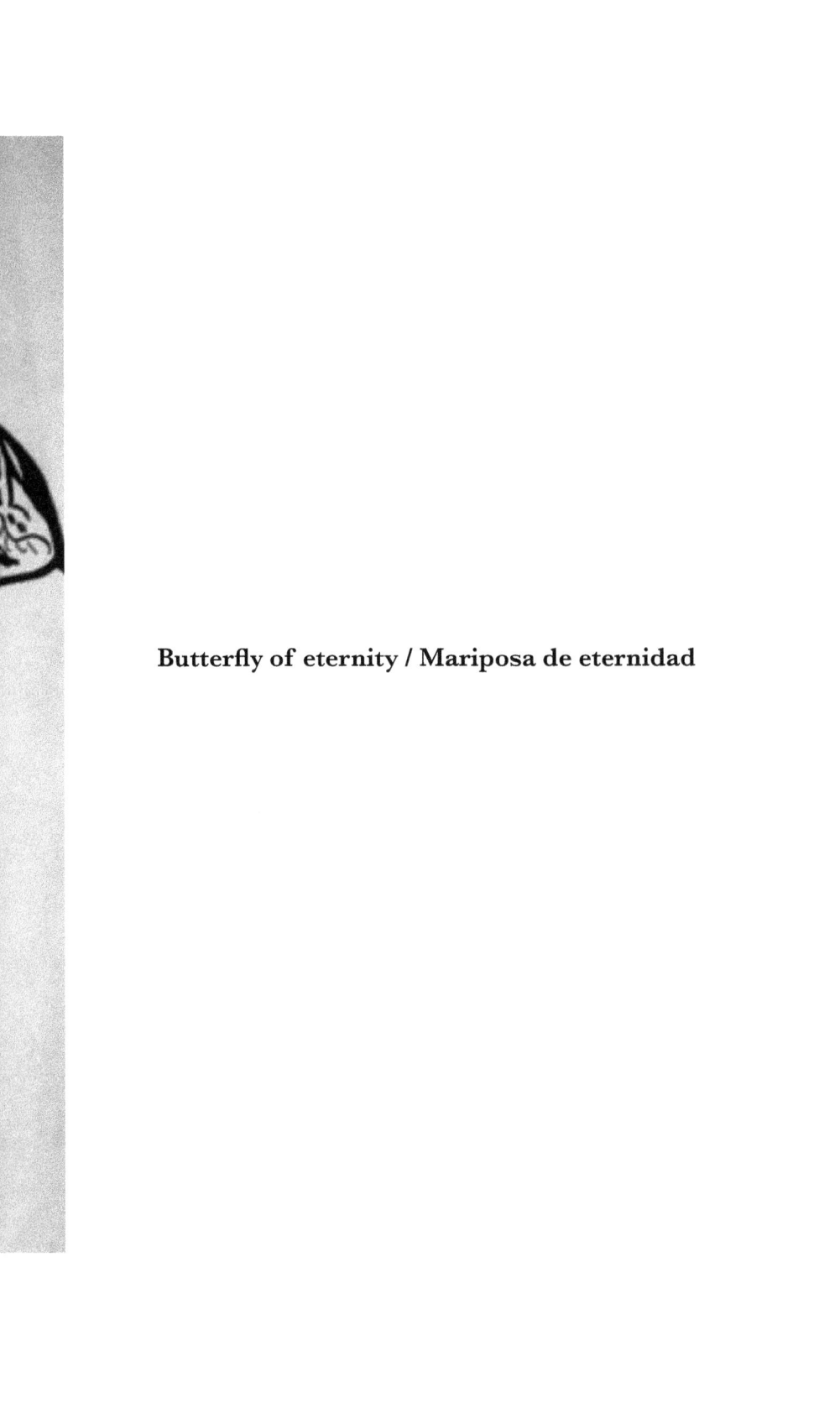

Butterfly of eternity / Mariposa de eternidad

III.
Spring: INTEGRATIONS

Faith and focus are a delight
I take flight

A fraction of instantaneous moments
Complete allowance
Freedom to roam!
To see
To be free

Pastures of energetic pallets
Harmonious action
Colors of interaction

Finding

Igniting

Initiating
Growing
Emanating

To radiate and

Translate

Feelings into thoughts

Thoughts to experiences

Building pools
Jumping in

Aligning with broader perspective
within

La fe y la concentración son un deleite
en el que tomo vuelo.

Una fracción de momentos instantáneos,
asignación completa.

Libertad para deambular,
para ver y ser libre.

Pasto de paletas energéticas,
acción armoniosa,
interacción de color rosa.

Descubrimiento.
Encendiendo.
Iniciando.
Creciendo.
Emanando.
Convirtiendo.

Sentimientos y pensamientos,
pensamientos y experiencias.

Construyendo piscinas,
saltando y entrando.

Alineando con perspectivas
más elevadas.

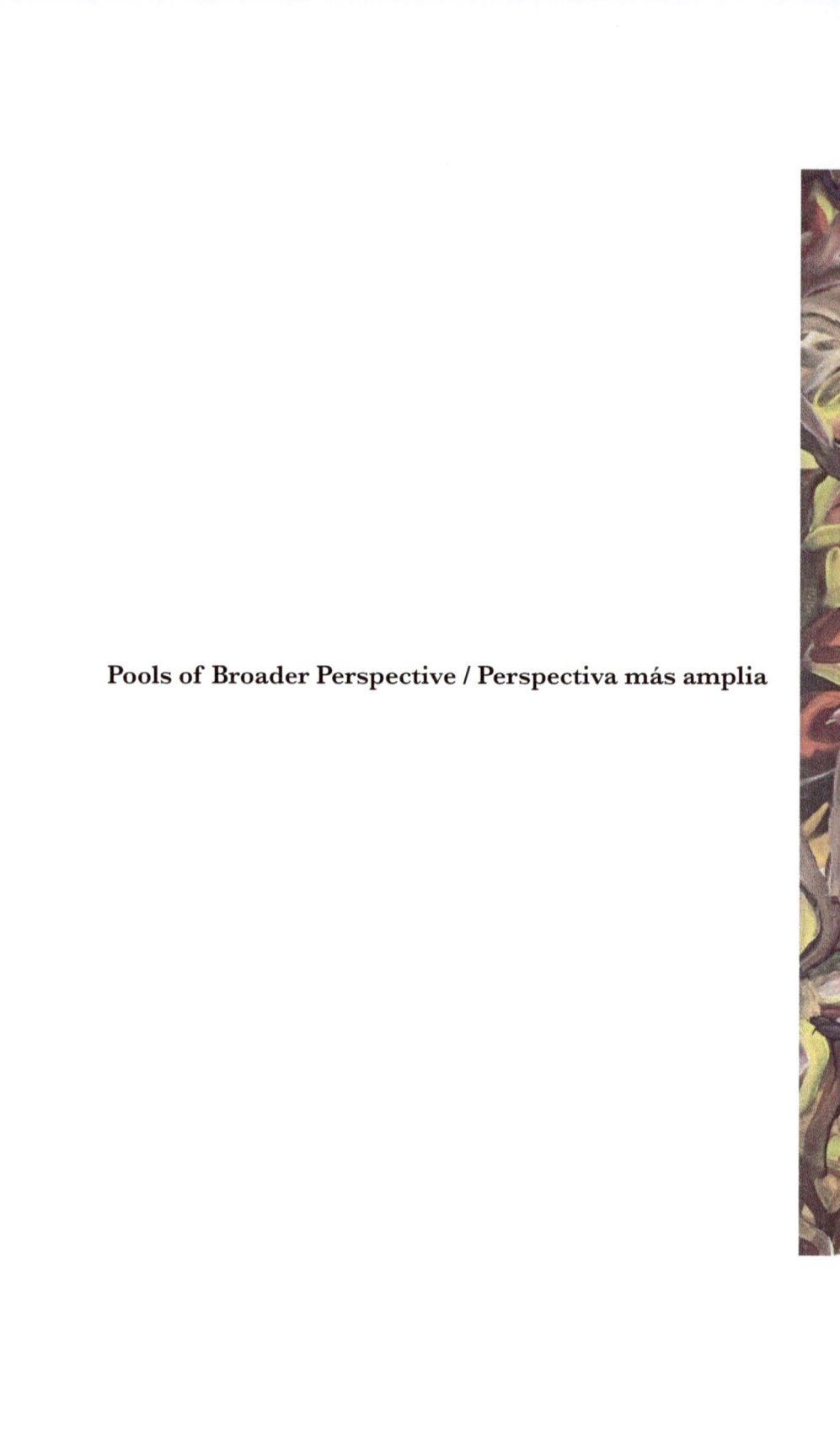

Pools of Broader Perspective / Perspectiva más amplia

Steady direction

       Allowing

          Flowing

            Transmuting

I, the conductor

              I, the illuminator

Essence of time-space
Thought and heart creating the lace

Vibrational reality
Consciousness in full vitality

 All that is
           harmonic transactions of desiring

 Elements of senses
          Feelings the distinguisher

 Antennae, the heart
            transmuter

 Higher perspective

          Composer

Dirección constante:

Permitiendo.

Fluyendo.

Transmutando.

Soy la conductora.

Soy la iluminadora.

Esencia del espacio-tiempo.

Pensamiento y corazón creando alineación.

Realidad vibratoria.

Conciencia de vitalidad plena.

Todo lo que son
transacciónes armónicas del deseo.

Elementos de los sentidos.
Sentimientos del destino.

Antenas del corazón.
Transmutar.

Perspectiva más alta.

Creadora.

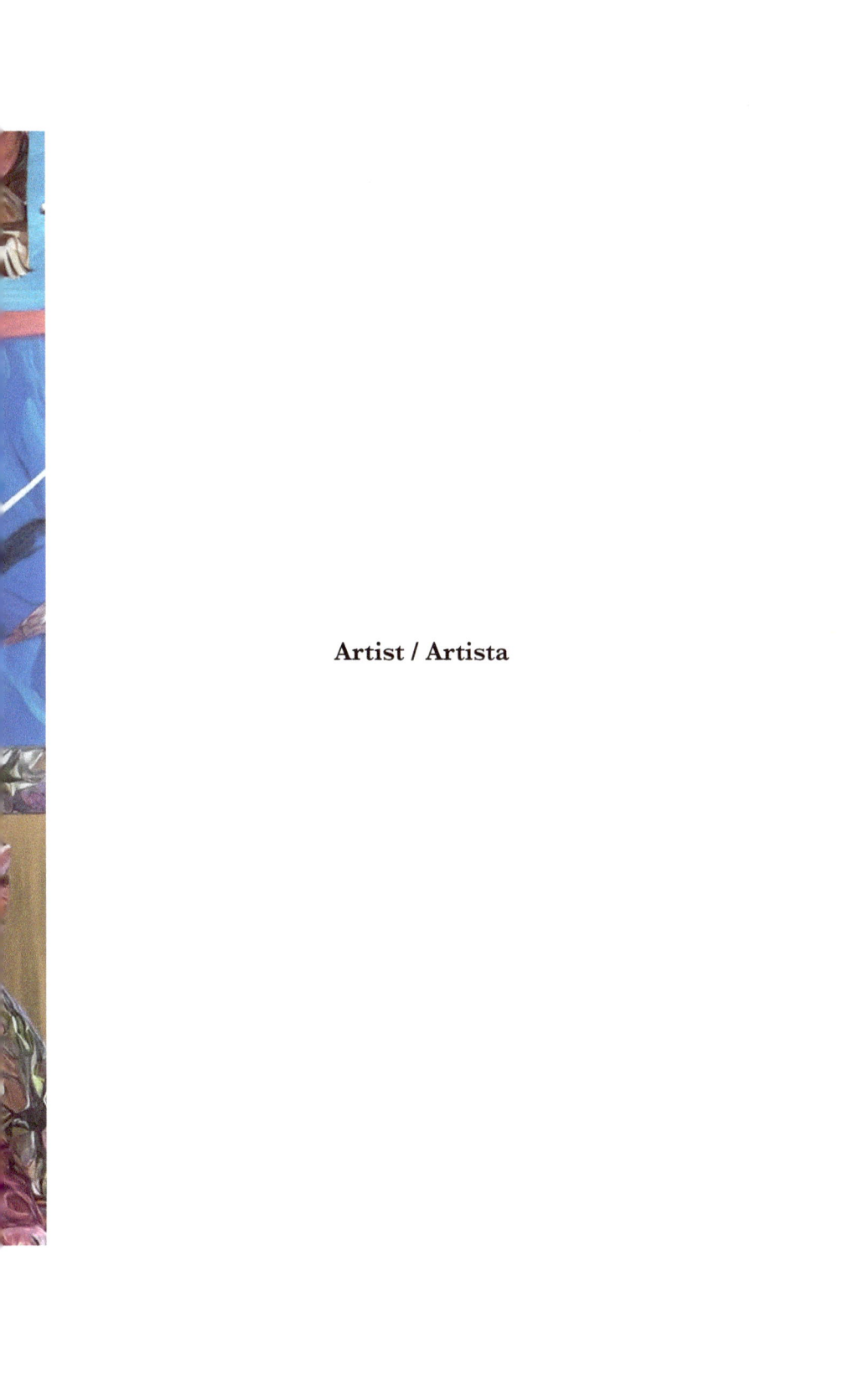

Artist / Artista

IV.
Spring: PRAYER

I call to the powerful direction of East, the wind, eagle, falcon
The one who holds the beacon
To the essence of the start of life
The one that illuminates the beginning of each day
Teach me to calm my mind, steady thy sails to ride the winds of the now
To trust, soar, and be free
Teach me to see clearly

I call to the igniting power of the direction of South,
fire, heat, passion, inspiration
The one who holds the flame
To the essence that allows me to dance through this game
The one who manifests the growth of who I become
As I stand and heal in the sun
Teach me
To breathe into the ember of my spirit so that I may truly be alive

I call to the infinite movement of the waters, direction of West,
oceans, rivers, lakes, snow, all that I know and don't know
The one who holds emotion
To the essence that allows me to experience notion,
direction, indication
The one who teaches me to float, to ride the wave, to be brave
Teach me to surrender, direct me to the right wave,
feeling into the right ways to behave

I call to the one I stand on, direction of North, Pachamama, plants,
rocks, mountains, trees, desserts, and all in between
The one who holds me, knowing I am seen
To the essence that creates structure, physical matter
The earth that gives me a ladder
The one who teaches me to anchor in thy roots and grow strong
Teach me to open thy heart knowing that I belong

A la poderosa dirección del Este,
al viento, al águila, al falcón.
Aire, brisa, viento y sensación.
A la esencia del comienzo de la vida,
dirección que ilumina el alba cada día.
Enséñame a calmar mi mente, a volar con la corriente.

A la poderosa dirección del Sur,
fuego, calor, pasión e inspiración.
La que sostiene la llama de la canción,
la esencia que me permite bailar a través del juego.
El que manifiesta el crecimiento, ¿en quién me convierto?
Flor, enséñame me a soplar las brasas de mi espíritu
para ser mi verdadero color.

Al poderoso infinito de las aguas del Oeste,
todo lo qué sé y lo qué no sé.
La capacidad de abrir la emoción,
la esencia que me permite experimentar noción,
dirección e indicación.
Enséñame a abrirme por dentro,
muéstrame cúando deba flotar, montar la ola o sentir el centro,
dirígeme al camino correcto
con mi corazón abierto.

A la poderosa dirección del Norte,
árboles, montañas, desiertos y todo lo demás.
Él que me aguanta.
Escncia que crea estructura,
la tierra, Madre, Diosa mía.
Él que me enseña a anclar mis raíces y crecer fuerte,
dame la fuerza para escalar a mis metas con suerte.

CHAPTER 3
SUMMER: EXPANSION

I.
Summer: POEMS OF CEREMONY

Heat rising
Blood boiling
Heart roaring

Sweat dripping
Breath deepening
Mind observing

Silence cleansing
Stillness transforming
Soul awakening

Beat immersing
Spine twirling
Hips grounding

Neck swaying
Arms lengthening
Feet rooting

Eckero singing
Aya guiding
Legs shaking

Sound leading
Soul dancing
Body receiving

Core engaging
Neck aligning
Arms flapping

Wind rushing
Strength rising
Dam unlocking

Fingers fluttering
Body moving
Central nervous system healing

Like moon shining
Is light glowing

Like sunburning
Is life unfolding

Aya showing

Muscles are fibers connecting
Bones are branches vibrating
Blood is water moving
Breath is air guiding
Mind is soul comprehending
Heart is the one connecting

El calor aumenta,
la sangre hierve,
el corazón ruge.

Goteo de sudor,
profunda respiración,
observo mi mente.

Purificación del silencio,
transformación de la quietud,
despertar del alma.

Inmersión en el ritmo,
giros de la columna,
enraizamiento de las caderas.

Balanceo del cuello,
estiramiento de los brazos,
enraizamiento de los pies.

Eckero cantando,
Aya guiando,
piernas temblando.

Sonidos llorando,
alma danzando,
cuerpo recibiendo.

Núcleo comprometido,
cuello alineado,
brazos aleteando.

Viento corriendo,
fuerza en aumento,
maldito desbloqueo.

Dedos agitados,
cuerpo en movimiento,
sistema nervioso central curando.

Brillando como la luna,
luz resplandeciente.
Quemando como el sol,
la vida desarrollándose.

Aya mostrando:
Los músculos son fibras que se conectan.
Los huesos son ramas que vibran.
La sangre es agua en movimiento.
La respiración es aire que guía.
La mente es alma que comprende.
El corazón es el que conecta.

Growing / Creciendo

Slithering like snake in grass
Energetic pull to break free at last
Swaying into circling
Weaving into my being

Directions to stand
Aya places my hands
Firm on the ground
Feet down to feel bound

I emerge like bark rooted so deep
To feel the power to be on my feet
Opening doors in my body
Joining into conscious reality

Tempo of sound, ignites, visual movement
Into all cracks and crevices of what needs to be disjointed

Tobacco holding space
The anointing of realization takes place
Conflict lives in illusion of perception
The false need to be victorious in confrontation

Heart grows stronger
Roots grow deeper
Releasing the need to perceive others
Is heat burning away debris that smothers

I shake, I rattle, I rumble
Breaking away densities of my temple
Steady in the breaking of consciousness
Releasing emotion from perception of blindness

Aya scans into the interactions of held emotions
Trapped by perceiving what others have done in situations
She gives me the choice to break the root
Or to live in the darkness of lost foot

I stand stronger in the decision to release
The old way of perceiving that brings disease
To break away and clear the root of judgment
Of what I see, I feel my legs, unlocking densities
So strong to shake away past memories

Right arm opening to heart of the sky
Left arm opening to the heart of the earth
Receiving deeper body experiencing energetic rebirth

Aya demonstrates the art of peace
Is kept when consciousness chooses ease
Strength in the standing tree
Is the force that connects awareness to see

From there, we move into reorganization
Body to higher dimension
New paradigm unlocked
New route to give life to what I desire to be cooking in my pot

Clarity, peace, prevail
Opening the veil
Demonstrations of light tentacles
Messages of I am important and humble are the scales

Harmonizing with angelic voice
I choose to dovetail the honest choice
Encoded with new nourishment of love
I am rooting and growing above

Giving deep thanks to the healing of the sacred Ayahuasca
For the conscious learning and teaching of Pachamama
As a pupil, disciple of the truth
I am equipped with the strength of strong roots...

Ritmo, moviendo cara y cuerpo,
deshaciendo y creciendo.
Yo me levanto.

Pies sobre la tierra,
anclando mis raíces,
medicina que me abre.

Siento mis venas, el agua es mi sangre.

Brazos abiertos
como el águila al viento.
Navegando por mi cerebro,
Aya apunta para descubrir algo.

La percepción de la gente es lo que confunde a la mente.
La emoción del mal entender atrapa a la fuente.
Memorias del pasado, cada transacción aguantando,
tomo la decisión de dejar ir el dado.

Crezco, ritmo con brinco,
ayudando a deshacer lo contaminado,
la consciencia que crea la percepción de todo,
la esencia de la raíz ahora cortada.

Mal entender,
queriendo poder
sobre circunstancias y conversaciones
que no nos dejan ver.
Terreno en movimiento, hojas cayendo, flores brotando,
densidad de emociones que se liberan.

Respiración profunda para soplar la duda,
meneando al ritmo, el cuerpo suda.
Amaneciendo a la verdad,
la paz es ver con tranquilidad.
Las piernas anclándose a una nueva realidad,
las células se estructuran como una nueva ciudad.
Cambiando consciencia para vivir en paz,
como un árbol creciendo mucho más.

Temple / Templo

Madre Tierra
Pachamama
Spirit of thy mother,
Creator

Ceremony begins
Heart feels strings
Beat of Earth,
Brought back to birth

Frequential alignment that allows for mind,
body, and spirit to join together
In perfect harmony
Like bee and honey
Cells opening wide to receive,
The nourishment, quantum ease

Clearing past medications,
Toxic ingredients released with Aya's indication,
Years of prescriptions wiped away
Radiant cells, new way

Kambo before cleared the path
So Aya could go in and do her math
Clean energetic cellular field
She enters deeper, I yield

Observing Aya's majestic dance
Feet aligned in stance
I feel her smile
Clearing energies of denial

Childhood molestation
Old white man violation
Cutting out the black seeds
Only Aya sees

Experiences of manipulation
Fragments of childhood stipulation
Days of in-school suspension
Fights to create protection

Aya shows me
Gives me the key
I feel, childhood somatic expression
Heart clearing recollection

Vibrating into a new dimension
Experiencing pure sensation
A new perspective, I lay
Protective ally here to stay

Shihuahuaco strength of thy tree
Allowing thy to be thee
Roots opening through feet
Trunk so strong within me

Arms like branches extending to receive
Hair is leaves telling story
The body is trunk, spiritual journey

Madre Tierra, Ayahuasca,
energía de fiesta.
Curandera alineándose a la frecuencia

Por dentro mi corazoncito
me aguanta / la siento,
yo la sigo.

Paso a paso con el ritmo,
juntas / bailando,
la conozco desde hace miles de años.

Paz por dentro, siento la elevación de mi pecho,
pulmones / expandiendo,
tranquilidad por dentro.

Soy un árbol de tronco grueso expandiendose para recibir paz,
Divina consciencia/ aprendiendo,
juntas somos el milagro.

La luz en la oscuridad.
La lluvia trae tranquilidad.
La verdad / la realidad.
La semilla que crece en la oscuridad.

New dimensions / Nuevas dimensiones

Inspiration
Divine motivation

Reconfigured consciousness set to new
It's I who is moving with you, aligned so true

Have peace of mind in this journey of life
Even if you don't have a husband or a wife

The old programming rooted in codependency
You are here to leave a legacy of independency

Surrender to the unknown
I am going to bless you with thy throne

Resources coming
Allies joining

Keep holding space
No such thing as a race

Be patient and enjoy the chapter
Thy story is continuously getting better

Inspiración, divina motivación.

Consciencia reconfigurada y puesta de nuevo.
Soy yo quien se mueve contigo, alineado acierto.

Tenga tranquilidad en este viaje de vida,
estás aprendiendo lo que necesitas.

La vieja programación arraigada es la codependencia,
estás aquí para dejar un legado de independencia,
entrégate a lo desconocido.
Voy a bendecirte con un trono.

Recursos que vienen uniéndose,
paso a paso mantienes el espacio.

Tu camino no es una carrera,
alinea tu frecuencia a la Tierra.
Ten paciencia y disfruta de los capítulos,
sigues creciendo.

The Story / La historia

II.
Summer: REALIZATIONS

Brilliant light
What a delight
To be in the energy of pure Sun frequency

The breeze
So sweet
Bee landing on feet

Green
Leaves like heart
Remembering source, and I never part

Zen
Full ten
Serenity that ignites intention

Full manifestation

Luz brillante,
¡qué delicia!
estar en la energía solar pura.

La brisa
tan dulce,
una abeja aterrizando sobre mis pies.

Verde,
la hoja es un corazón.
Recordando la fuente, yo nunca me separo.

Zen
al cien.
Serenidad que enciende la intención.

Manifestación pura.

Sun / Sol

What we plant is what we grow
That's why it's important to know

What we think is what we become
That's why it's important to receive heart wisdom

Fulfillment of truth
That lives in the heart of thy youth

Synergistically lighting the fire
Hearts deepest desire

That we planted inside
Where source knew it could hide

Intergalactic, universal expansiveness
This genius is rooted in masterfulness

Cup half full
Knowing that life is beautiful

The capacity to grow, to be transitional
Truth is exponential

Know inner purity
Darkness is light inside, ingenuity

Acceptance of it all
Unlocks and brings down the walls

New perceptions with new extensions
That create positive momentum

Unlaced to unpack the old
Once was dark there's now gold

Climbing to new heights
New challenges ignite

The strength that it took to climb
Gives thee remembrance that all is fine

Like grapes on a vine
Turn to wine

The running turns into an unexpected fall
Where something needed to shift to create a new hall

Aspects of life and light are one
Growing under the Sun

En aquello que pensamos, nos convertimos.
Por eso es importante recibir la sabiduría del corazón.

Cumplimiento de la verdad
que vive en el corazón de tu juventud.

Encendiendo el fuego sinérgicamente
a los deseos más profundos del corazón.

¿Qué plantamos por dentro que
sabía que podía esconderse?

Expansión intergaláctica y universal,
este genio tiene sus raíces en la maestría.

Taza medio llena
saber que la vida es bella.

La capacidad de crecer, ser, transicionar.
La verdad es exponencial.

Conoce la pureza interior,
la oscuridad es luz por dentro.

La aceptación de todo
desbloquea y derriba las paredes.

Nuevas percepciones con nuevas extensiones
que crean un impulso positivo.

Sin cordón para desempacar la vieja realidad...
Alguna vez estuvo oscuro, ahora hay oro.

Subiendo a nuevas alturas
se encienden nuevos desafíos.

La fuerza que hizo falta para subir,
te recuerda que todo está bien.

Como uvas en la vid,
recurrir al vino.

La carrera se convierte en una caída inesperada
donde algo necesitaba cambiar para crear una nueva sala.

Los aspectos de la vida y la luz son uno
creciendo bajo el sol divino.

Paradigm Grid / Cuadrícula de paradigmas

Receiving the new
Destination
Followed by deep transformation
Healing the hurt of deeper manifestation
The karmic dimension

Receiving the new
Held with love through heart connections
Letting go of all painful emotions
Rocked with compassion to heal all demons
Becoming best friends through these transactions

Receiving the new
Heart, soul heals, reveals
Wisdom that unveils
Breaks down the rails
Unhooks the nails

Receiving the new
Clearing the walls
Opening the halls
Dissolving the dust
Transforming the lust

Receiving the new
Burning the rage
Washing away the cage
Heart breaks free
Now it's easier to see

Receiving the new
Guidance with each step
Rocks on a riverbed, healed head
Allowing heart to be the GPS
Releasing the minds need to create stress

Receiving the new
Accepting the greatness of life
Consciousness sharp like knife
We are safe where we are going
The discomfort is in the illusion of not knowing

Receiving the new...

Recibiendo lo nuevo.
Destino seguido de una profunda transformación,
sanando el dolor de una profunda manifestación,
las dimensiones kármicas.

Recibiendo lo nuevo.
Sostenido con amor a través de conexiones del corazón,
dejar ir todas las emociones dolorosas,
compasión para sanar a todos los demonios,
convertirse en mejores amigos con la ayuda de estas transacciones.

Recibiendo lo nuevo.
Corazón, alma sana, revela,
sabiduría que desvela.
Rompe los rieles,
desengancha los clavos.

Recibiendo lo nuevo.
Quemando la rabia.
Quitándose la jaula.
Corazón en libertad.
Ahora es más fácil de ver.

Recibiendo lo nuevo.
Orientación en cada paso,
rocas en el lecho de un río, cabeza curada.
Permitiendo que el corazón sea el GPS,
liberar la necesidad de crear estrés.

Recibiendo lo nuevo.
Aceptar la grandeza de la vida.
Consciencia afilada como un cuchillo.
Estamos seguros a dónde vamos,
el malestar está en la ilusión de no saber.

New vision / Nueva visión

Evergreen, the essences of heart
We sometimes forget, but never part

The stream of nourishment kept when mind aligns to heart
Guiding the actions that lead to a new start

Living in the now
Where it all matters no need to know how

Just allowing
For the flowing

The constant developing
The healing

Remembering
Transforming

The cycle that becomes the past, bringing the new
Establishing the renewed

Becoming one with the beat
Fire in heart creating heat

Stillness kept in breath
Soothing the feelings of depth

That keeps me warm
In the cold deep waters

Where all is reborn...

Evergreen las esencias del corazón,
a veces nos olvidamos pero nunca nos separamos.

El flujo de alimento se mantiene cuando la mente se alinea con el
corazón,
guiando las acciónes que conducen a un nuevo comienzo.

Viviendo en el ahora,
donde todo importa y no hay necesidad de saberlo.

Solo permitiéndolo
para el que fluye.

El constante desarrollo
es la curación.

Recordando,
transformando.

El ciclo que se convierte en pasado trayendo lo nuevo,
estableciendo la renovada.

Convertirse en uno con el ritmo.
Fuego en el corazón creando calor.

Quietud mantenida en la respiración.
Calmando los sentimientos desde la profundidad.

Eso me mantiene caliente
en las frías y profundas aguas.

En donde todo renace.

Reborn / Renaciendo

Going through shifts
Like water in a river / it hits
Hard
Then softens / passes
Changes are constantly flowing like wind in the grass
To break the stem / release the seed
The cycle lives in growing indeed

Pasando por cambios
como agua en un río / golpea duro,
luego se suaviza / pasa...

Los cambios fluyen constantemente como el viento en la hierba,
romper el tallo / soltar la semilla.
El ciclo vive en crecer de hecho.

Cycles / Ciclos

III.
Summer: INTEGRATIONS

Money they say matters
The undertaking of society's ladders

They also say money is time
Like lemonade is to lime

Aya says time is the moment
And the present equates to enjoyment

Earth's field, the bank
Conscious awareness is the tank

Play in thy abundance in full employment
So that heart creates frequency of enjoyment

Synergistic waves of anointment
Letting go of illusions of opponent

Impoverished mind deteriorates
New recognition vibrates

Reprogramming
Expanding
Garden growing...

Dicen que el dinero importa,
el emprendimiento de la sociedad.

Dicen que el dinero es tiempo,
como la limonada es a la lima.

Aya dice que tiempo es el momento,
el presente equivale a disfrutar.

El campo de la Tierra, el banco.
La consciencia presente, el tanque.

Juega con la abundancia en el pleno empleo,
para que el corazón cree frecuencia de alegría.

Ondas sinérgeticas de unión,
dejar ir las ilusiones del oponente.

La mente empobrecida se deteriora,
el nuevo reconocimiento vibra.

Reprogramación
en expansión.

La consciencia es la mansión.

Expanding / Expandiendo

Jackie Guerra

Waters of plenty
Bathing / richness of many

Higher awareness like soaring eagle
Steady / thy trickle

Becoming thy stream
Manifesting / biggest dream

Living in the blue
Infinite space / hue

Defining soulful mission
Collective realities / full vision

Transitioning and changing
Constantly / transcending

Agua de abundancia,
baño / riqueza de muchas.

Mayor conciencia como el águila volando,
constante / tu chorrito.

Convertirse en tu corriente,
manifestando / un sueño más grande.

Viviendo en el azul,
espacio infinito / tono.

Definiendo una misión conmovedora,
realidades colectivas / visión completa.

Transición y movimiento,
constantemente / trascendiendo.

Transcending / Trascendiendo

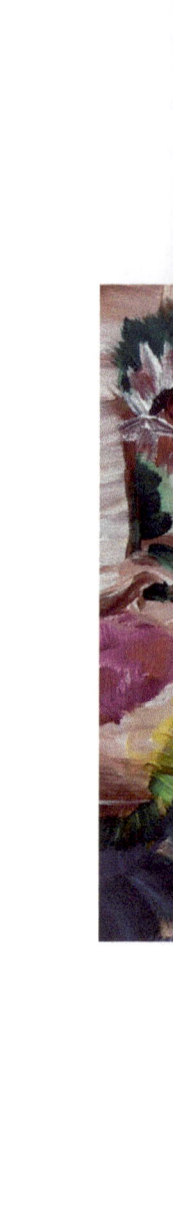

She
Unlimited abundance seen and unseen
The transfer of worthiness enters like light beam
Core of awakened being

She
Roots in multiple directions
Anchoring lessons
Prosperity comes in many dimensions

She
Drawing from thy stream of abundance
Learning that all is remembrance
Choosing thought patterns that align with feeling of sustenance

She
Creating the space to see the ocean of infinity
The vastness in Earth's wellness and beauty
Her abundance growing infinitely

She
Unleashing the hundreds of years of truth like a dam
Opening floodgates to origin of woman
How Earth started and how it all began

She
The leader
He, the maker
We, the creator

She
The birth giver
Life generator
The master

She
The queen bee
Male and female see
Hive lives in harmony

Ella,
abundancia ilimitada.
La transferencia del merecimiento de luz, ilumina.
Núcleo del ser despierta.

Ella,
raíces en múltiples direcciones,
anclando las lesiones.
La prosperidad viene en varias dimensiones.

Ella,
recibiendo desde la fuente de abundancia,
aprendiendo que todo es memoria,
escogiendo formas de ser alineadas con el sentido de sustancia.

Ella,
creando espacio para ver el océano infinito.
La grandeza de ver el bienestar y lo bello
para que la abundancia crezca hasta el cielo.

Ella,
abriendo la presa de agua,
recibiendo en compuertas al origen de la mujer.
¿Cómo empezó la tierra?

Ella,
la lider.
Él
el constructor.
Nosotros, los creadores.

Ella,
dadora de nacimiento.
Generadora de vida y crecimiento.
El maestro.

Ella,
la abeja reina.
Macho y hembra ven
la colmena que vive en armonía.

Goddess of Fertility / Diosa de la fertilidad

IV.
Summer: PRAYER

Wings of colors
Bring me higher

Teach me to let go to expand
Creating space
To receive all that allows for growth

Vividly live, fly, swiftly glide
Allow focus to turn and shift to continue to ride

Alas de colores,
llévenme a lo alto.

Enséñame a dejar ir lo que no necesito,
creando el espacio
para recibir todo lo que me permite crecer.

Expandir, vivir y volar;
enfocándome para cambiar.

Great Spirit, Mother Earth, Dearest Sun, and Awakening Moon
Affirm deep within my heart so that the echo of thy love rings
through the chambers of Thy mind to ignite the thoughts that

I love waking up and being alive
I am so grateful for how I feel inside
Perfect health
Receiving lots of wealth
Aligned with source
Powerful force
Breathing deep throughout the morning
Every evening
Allowing the presence of spirit
To be intertwined with each movement
I am choosing to be open to what is in alignment
Releasing the need to be stagnate

I am flowing
Face, body, aura glowing
Heart strong
Knowing I belong
Attracting positive experiences
New partnerships
Golden opportunities
Divine prosperity
Every second aware of breath
Connected to thy depth
Vibrant bold and true
I am one with thy hue
Thy light
I am divine clarity and insight

Gran espíritu, Madre Tierra, querido Sol y Diosa Luna,
afirmó en lo profundo de mi corazón para que el eco de su amor
resuene por mi vida:
¡Me encanta despertar y estar viva!

Estoy tan agradecida por lo que siento por dentro:
Perfecta salud en armonía
y recibir toda la riqueza.

Alineada con la fuente,
fuerza poderosa,
respiro profundo durante todas las mañanas
y todas las noches.
Permitir la presencia del espíritu,
entrelazada con cada movimiento,
estoy eligiendo abrirme a las sorpresas.
Liberar la necesidad de estar estancada.

Fluyendo,
cara, cuerpo, aura resplandeciente,
corazon fuerte...
Sé cómo dirigir la mente:
recibiendo experiencias positivas,
nuevas asociaciones,
oportunidades de oro,
prosperidad divina.

Cada segundo consciente de la respiración,
vibrante, atrevida y verdadera.
Soy uno con el todo,
soy la luz,
soy claridad y perspicacia divina.

CHAPTER 4
FALL : ANCESTRAL

I
Fall : POEMS OF CEREMONY

Steady
Slow
Sensation felt below

Undertow
Currents that shape thy flow
Brings breath to grow

Aya enters so gently
Seeping into crevices shining lightly
Into blockages that keep thee from feeling mighty

Remembrances consciousness carries
Moments that vary
Perceptions of what is "scary"

Childhood rejection
Aya uses her detection
Pulls out the files for recollection

One by one, I see
Forgive, let go
Understanding the beliefs that don't let confidence flow

Age by age, grade by grade
Step by step
Aya guides thee through the depth

Hitting rock bottom
Thy lowest of lows
Deep breath, allowing pain to overflow

Like dirty sponge being squeezed
Letting it all bleed
Strong vines pushing out dark seeds

Surrendering to volcano of shame
Ideologies of fame
Burning through stagnant energies with her flame

Sitting in harmony
Observing the sponge clear and empty
Slowly accepting the vast space, new capacity

Open pasture
Space for pleasure
New consciousness that remembers

The essence, beauty of all that I am
Ayahuasca opens the dam
To the purity of woman

Dancing together in Aya's song
I made it!
With ancient energies that come along

Happiness, confidence
Strength, perseverance
Ayahuasca gives thee remembrance

Entrando suavemente,
sintiendo la corriente
de la linda medicina, se siente.

La importancia de las memorias de mi niñez,
cómo lo que me dijeron afectó mi pensamiento,
Aya me aguanta mientras nos miramos, se vive.

Las películas y memorias de dolor.
En cada relación de "amor"
aprendí a no tener valor.

Año con año,
grado por grado,
Aya me exprime igual que a un sucio paño.

Energías y pensamientos no alineados a la consciencia divina,
rafaga de emociones expulsadas
con la fuerza de Madre Tierra.

Lloro.
La siento.
Dejo ir todo entre mis lágrimas de cielo.

Entendiendo qué es lo que me limitaba.
Abro un espacio
nuevo y sincero.

Reconozco la confianza de nuevo,
cncrgía podcrosa como el viento
que mueve todo.

Fiesta con canciones de plantas que me enseñan
cómo navegar como una estrella en medio de la oscuridad.
Y tener gracia por ser bella.

Bailando con el ritmo de Madre Tierra,
abuelita, amiguita, Ayahuasca,
Diosa Mía.

Open Dam / Presa abierta

Space created, she's flowing in
Like waters clearing sin

The illusions of thy mind, old consciousness releasing within
Breathing in

Seeing depth of thy intricate beauty
In her delicate fruits of sexuality

The vagina of creation
Thy mothers manifestation

Infinite sacred geometric corridor
Sequential all in order

Quantum arms infinite legs
Quantum threads

Intertwining, creating, moving, living
Weaving

Movement in every crevice inside
I contract, I open, I die

Taken to past life where I created stronghold
Undoing the learning that created mold

he thoughts before death is what is remembered
In the deepest parts of spirit where it is chambered

Aya opens the corridors to moments locked in ancient past
Where I was queen, Indigenous, and protected my tribe thinking it
would last

Foreign, white faces,
Loud guns, shooting at our faces

Memory unlocked in Aya's arms
I feel thy heart beat like alarms

Right shoulder numbs, neck spasms
I feel a blow to my abdomen

I see my tribe being demolished
As the soldiers hold me captive

I die slowly, thinking, "How could this happen?"
I am the queen, I couldn't protect them, what is my lesson?

I see the darkness of those thoughts appear
Aya holds me as she starts to clear

I forgive the soldiers for introducing fear
Shedding deep tears

The karmic energies of the past
Memories of indigenous life flooding in at last

Where thy land was thy teacher
The sun, thy preacher

The stars thy leader
Ayahuasca thy commander

The moon thy weaver
Thy feelings thy weather

I feel thy shoulder break free
Thy neck transformed into lengthened harmony

Thy abdomen
Renewed, feeling whole again

Aya lives in every tissue
Healing every issue

Tobacco smoke comes to clear the remnants
Of past tears that hardened thy sentiment

Agua florida over thy crown
The flowers healing frown

Like leaves falling from tree
I had to die to break free

Esencia pura por dentro,
llena de energía y movimiento.

Corriendo por mis venas y mis células;
tranquila, respira, disfruta el momento.

La dejo, Aya me lleva
abriendo mis ojitos lindos.

Viendo los detalles,
infinitos momentos de ocio.

Colores y flores cautivando el centro.
Sus manitos, infinitos.

Su belleza tan grande
abriéndome por la sangre.

En cada célula, las moléculas,
las energías, detalles.

Aya me dice que voy a morir
para descubrir.

Las experiencias que dejaron cicatrices
en las partes más profundas.
La fábrica de mi alma, tejiendo quién soy.

Aya abre las puertas de los momentos
que en mi espíritu quedaron atrapados afectando mi mente.
Cuando yo era reina, indigena, protectora de mi gente,
pensando que todo estaría bien para siempre.

Extranjeros, caras blancas
disparando pistolas a nuestras caras.

Memoria descubierta en Aya's manos,
mi corazón comenzando con fuertes latidos.

Hombro derecho entumecido, mi cuello siente un espasmo.
También un golpe a él abdominal,
viendo que este es el final
de mi gente, de mi tribu.

Los soldados aguantándome para que yo mire.
Mi tribu moriendose.

Muero despacio,
ese momento en el que pienso:

"Gran espíritu, ¿cómo puedes dejar esto pasar?".
"Yo soy la reina de la paz y dejastes a los blancos ganar".

Veo la oscuridad de esa memoria aparecer,
Aya me contiene para limpiar lo que no me deja crecer.

Perdono a los soldados,
a las personas que nos mataron.

Nuevas puertas se abren,
luz y dice, vengan.

Energías kármicas del pasado,
memorias indígenas lindas y el origen.

Donde la tierra era maestra
y el sol predicador.

Las estrellas enseñando lo venidero,
Aya comandante.

La luna tejedora,
las emociones, el clima.

Siento mi hombro romperse, liberarse,
mi cuello transformado armonía alargada
en nueva sangre.

Mi abdomen renovado,
sintiéndose completo de nuevo.

Aya vive en cada tejido
sanándolo todo.

El humo del tabaco viene a limpiar la remanencia
de lágrimas pasadas que endurecieron en la consciencia.

Agua de flores respirada por encima,
mi corazón dando gracias.

Como las hojas que caen del árbol,
también tuve que morir para ver el sol.

Indigenous self / Yo indígena

II.
Fall : REALIZATIONS

Jackie Guerra

Bark is rainbow bridge
Mossy green with branch like hinge
Leaves, singe

Growing like vapers
Elemental skyscrapers
Earth's ancient commentators

Cylindrical yet pentagonal
Visual felt spiritual
Vertical grounded horizontal

Masterpieces are environmental

Ladra como un puente arcoíris,
verde musgo con bisagras en forma de ramas.
Hojas, Tiziano, chamuscar.

Creciendo como vapeadores,
rascacielos elementales.
Antigua de la tierra.

Cilíndrica pero pentagonal.
Sentida, visual y espiritual.
Vertical puesto a tierra horizontal.

Las obras maestras son ambientales.

Masterpiece is Earth / La obra maestra es Madre Tierra

Jackie Guerra

Thy body her palace
She is thy queen
I thy temple

She shows how opening can be so simple

Nourishment / seed
Sweetness / in honey
Cherishing / the dance

Differentiation of love in romance...

Body is fire / needing air
Rooted / in Earth
Nourished / by water

It's all part

of the

infinite circle

Mi cuerpo es su palacio.
Ella es la reina de cuerpo,
semilla y alimento.

Dulzura / en la miel.
Sensación / en la piel.
Apreciando / el baile.
Disfrutando / aire.

Arraigado en la tierra,
nutrido por el agua,
el cuerpo es fuego,
calentando y a la vez dejando.

Creciendo
y también
derramando.

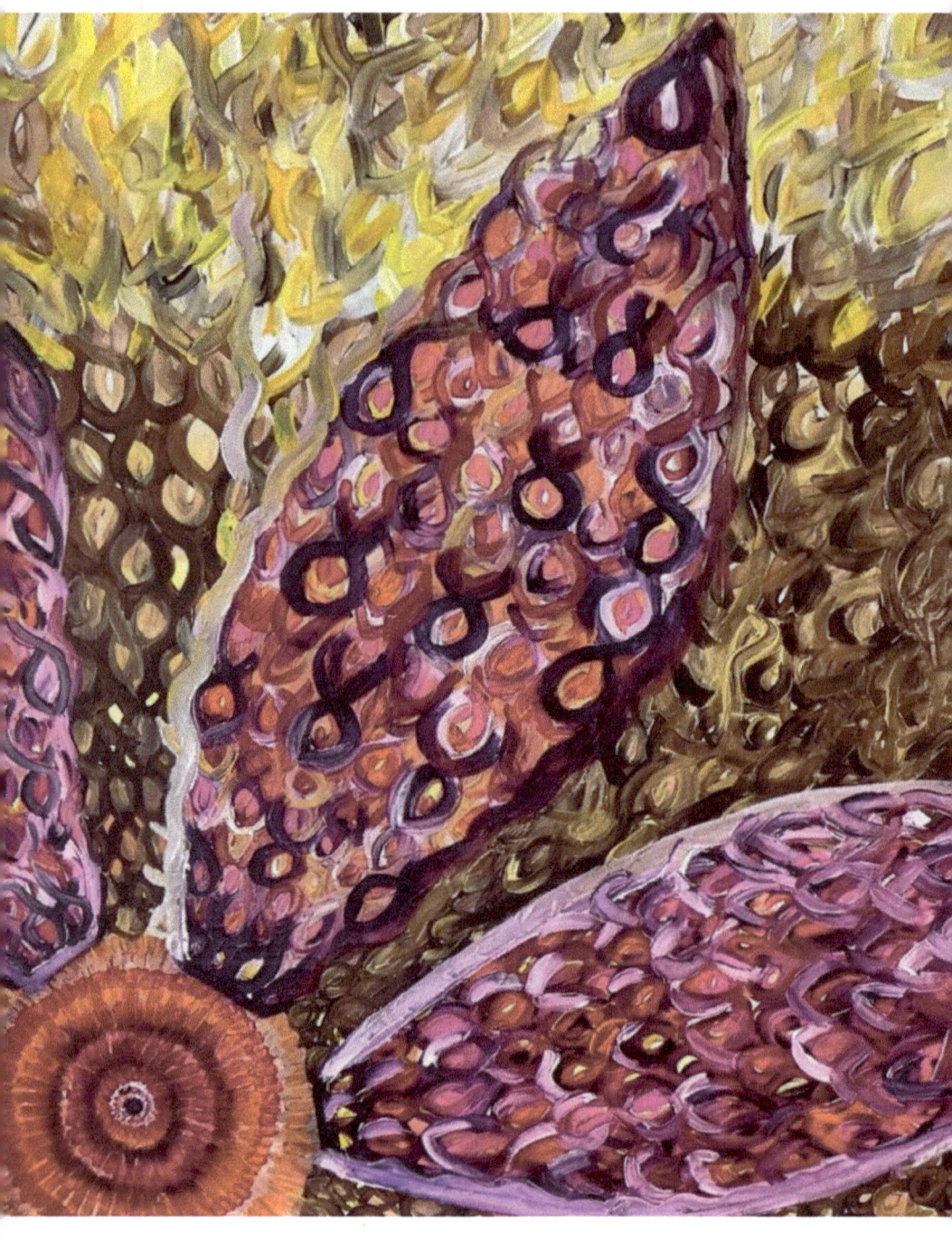

Infinite / Infinito

III.
Fall : INTEGRATIONS

Waves of cold air
Amongst the lightness that dares
To break through the darkness that stares

Into the truth of what is
Allowing for illusion to dismiss
The courage it takes to allow the shadow to surface
Is the wisdom of light from the crevice

Conjuring the peace within to anchor
To release and simmer
Like cold in the warmth
Or sunshine with its rains
There is power in washing away the pain...

Como olas de aire frío,
entre la ligereza que se atreve
a atravesar la oscuridad que mira.

En la verdad de lo qué es,
permitiendo que la ilusión se desestime
a atravesar la oscuridad que mira.

En la verdad del espejo,
permitiendo que la ilusión se desestime.
El coraje se necesita para permitir que la sombra salga,
es la sabiduría de la luz en la grieta.

Conjurando la paz interior para anclar,
soltar y cocer a fuego lento,
como el frío en el calor,
como los rayos del sol cuando llueve.
Hay poder en lavar el dolor.

Light from the crevice / Luz de las grietas

Having fun with it all

Crawl

Stumble

To stand the lesson of thy land

Honoring quantum intelligence

Strength in her vigilance

Creating space to rest
Reset
To observe
In honor of her

Clarity instead of blur
Ready to be tree
Fertile soil's fertility
Roots anchored in loyalty
Base like a boulder
Emerging into quantum heights as I get older

Divirtiéndome con todo.

Gatear.

Tropezar.

Parar.

Las lecciones de la tierra
honrando a la inteligencia cuántica.
Fuerza en su vigilancia.

Creando espacio para descansar,
reiniciar, sanar...
Observar es honrarla a ella.

Claridad en lugar del desenfoque.
Listo para ser árbol.
Suelo fértil.

Raíces ancladas en lealtad,
la base es de roca anclada.
Emergiendo a alturas cuánticas a medida que envejezco.

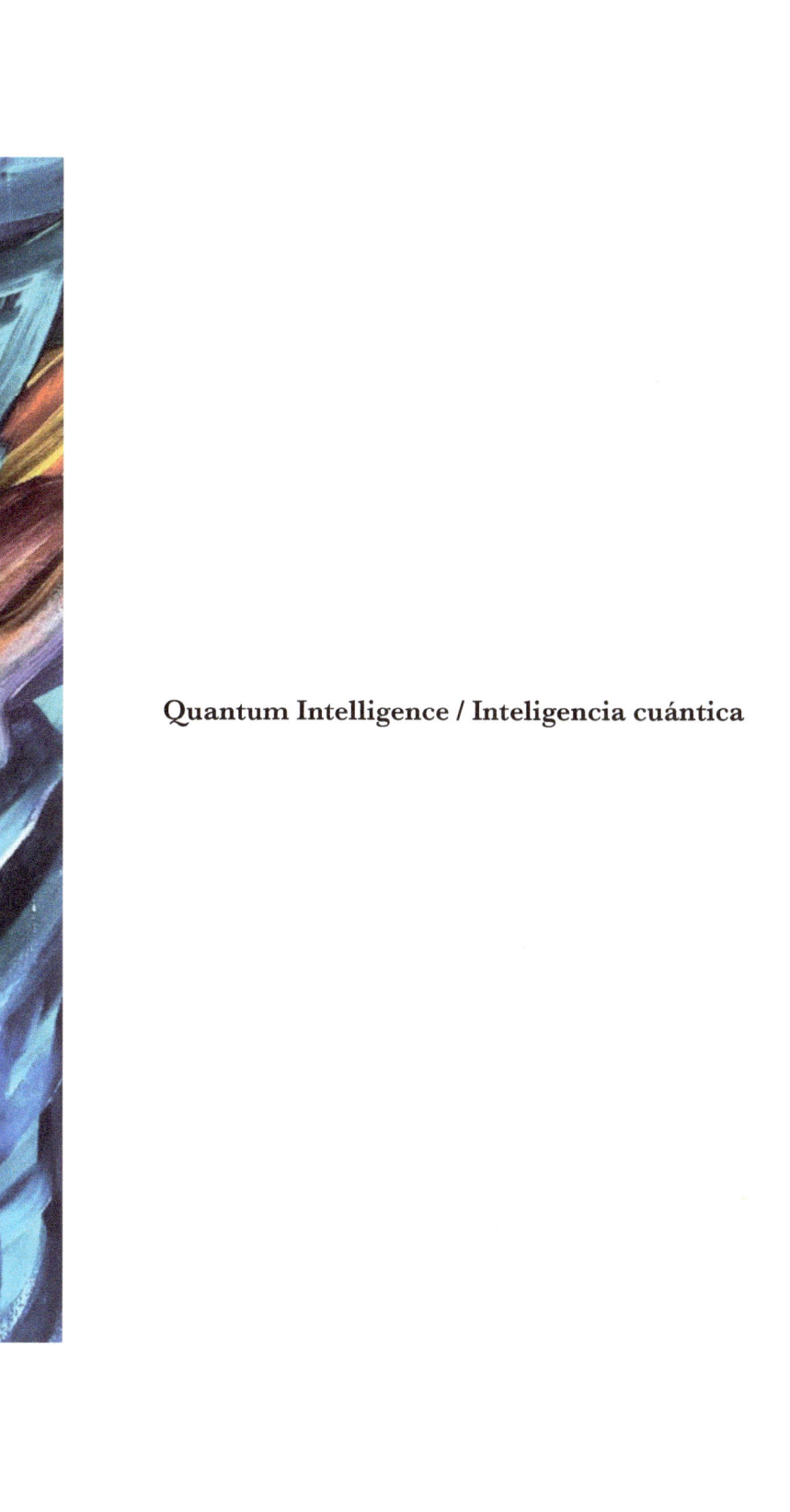

Quantum Intelligence / Inteligencia cuántica

Known inside
Higher and higher states
This is where real treasures reside

Obscure mind detaches
Burns away
Spirit lighting the matches

Blowing into ember
Trust
Feeling the heat I remember

The change inside
Evolve
Its time, morphing tide

Core opened
Rooted
Deepened

Softening
Opening of thy heart
Resolving

Awareness
Now
New states of consciousness

Flowing time
Masterful mosaic
Creating own rhyme

Free of judgment
Blessing with love
No need to resent

Focusing on present
Leading to then
Exploring sentiment

Unfolding reality to plow
I, tools
New space to live in the now

Earth, wife
Married
Creating advanced life

Transforming to experience and see
Leaves falling
Higher versions of thee

Conociendo por dentro
estados cada vez más altos.
Aquí es donde residen los verdaderos tesoros.

La mente oscura se separa,
se quema.
Espíritu encendiendo las cerillas.

Soplando las brasas,
confianza.
Sintiendo el calor, recuerdo.

El cambio interior,
evolucionar.
Es hora, flujos del ambiente,
marea cambiante.

Núcleo abierto,
enraizado,
profundo.

Ablandamiento,
apertura de corazón.
Resolviendo.

Conocimiento
ahora.
Nuevos estados de consciencia.

El tiempo fluye,
mosaico magistral
creando su propia rima.

Sin juicio,
bendición con amor.
No hay necesidad de resentirse.

Centrándose en el presente,
conduciendo hacia el futuro,
explorando el sentimiento.

Desplegando la realidad para arar.
Yo, la herramienta.
Nuevo espacio para vivir el ahora.

Tierra, esposa
casada.
Creando vida avanzada.

Transformando para experimentar y ver
las hojas cayendo.
Versiones superiores de mí.

Higher version / Versión más alta

IV.
Fall : PRAYER

I love all that I am

All that I am becoming

I am letting go, then surrendering

Trusting that everything is happening in divine timing

I am protected

I create the space to be well-rested

I speak from thy heart

Allowing the essence of thee to be the art

Appreciation for the shedding of old leaves

For the process is creating so the heart sees

The new space there is to create

I know what I am living is truly great

I am feeling at peace

I am riding with ease

Amo todo lo que soy.

Amo en quién me estoy convirtiendo.

Entregándome, me estoy soltando.

Confiar en que todo sucede en el tiempo divino.

Estoy protegida.

Creo el espacio para estar bien descansada.

Hablo de corazón.

Permitiendo que la esencia de mí sea el arte.

Agradeciendo por el desprendimiento de las hojas viejas.

El nuevo espacio que hay para crear.

La libertad para volar.

Estoy viviendo, ¡es realmente genial!

Me siento en paz.

Estoy viviendo con facilidad.

Acknowledgements

Deep appreciation for Carlos Arias, my best friend who brought me to the medicine. I am thankful for your love for Aya and your guidance while practicing.

Deep gratitude to the Ashaninka people of Peru in the Mayantuyacu lineage of Maestro Juan Flores Salazar for the incredible essence of the medicine, the plants, and ecosystem that hold the sacred energies to produce these plants, these sacred medicines, and who are so generous with showing the way.

Deep thanks to Dana Kittrelle, my Hakomi therapist and partner in integration. Thank you for all your wisdom, support, and love. Your voice and guidance has been the sacred key to creating a safe space so I can go into the darkest parts of self. I wouldn't be where I am today without your perspective, love, and support.

Thank you to Jimmy Castillo, my Kambo practitioner who has assisted me in clearing the path so Aya could go in and do her math. So thankful for the way you carry the medicine with so much intention, integrity, and love.

Thank you to Nacho Arimany for being a masterful teacher. Thank you for teaching me how to use my voice as an instrument of the universe to positively impact others.

Thank you to Claudia Bumuller for taking the time to bless me with deep reiki healing and sound baths. I appreciate all the times you made yourself available to make sure I received the healing sessions in preparation for the ceremony.

Thank you to Brian Koerner for carrying Kambo medicine with so much integrity. I appreciate the space you've held in the most physically challenging moments. I appreciate all you've done for me.

Thank you to Tatiana Aya Tupinambá, for such deep healing journeys with the sacred medicine. Thank you for being such a strong light in the darkest of spaces. Thank you for your sacred songs and devotion. Your practice is what sparked my deep love for Ayahuasca.

Thank you to Angelica Aguilera, my creative editor and poetry coach who has been a key piece to my creative process in getting all my journals to manuscript status. I appreciate your lens so much.

Thank you to Davina Ferreira for believing in me, giving me a platform to publish, and for the safe space to create.

Get to Know Jackie M Guerra

Jackie Guerra is a visionary leader in the world of fitness and athletic engineering. Her accomplishments as a trailblazing Olympic athlete in women's soccer, and as a health educator, innovator, and entrepreneur have made her one of the sports and fitness industry's most sought-after advisors and trainers. A Plano, Texas native of Puerto Rican decent, Guerra was a Varsity soccer player at the

University of Illinois Urb. Champaign, where she graduated with bachelor's degrees in Applied Health Sciences. Later to receive her Masters in Kinesiology. Guerra's professional journey began during her years as a competitive collegiate athlete: responding to the rigors of her competitive sports regimen, Guerra embarked on an extensive research program to improve her level of fitness by conducting independent studies on heart rate variability and energy system development on female soccer players, which formed the foundation of her methodology: the Theory of Optimal Fitness (TOF). While still a student, Guerra created specialized conditioning programs for the entire University of Illinois women's soccer team; excellent preparation for doing the same for the USA U-21 Women's National Soccer Team prior to the World Cup. As a four-year NCAA letter winner who set the longest winning streak in Illinois history, Guerra led her team to win the Big 10 Conference title.

In 2017, Guerra took her genius TOF methodology a few steps further by developing empirically-based, position-specific curriculum for NBA, MLS & NWSL players. She continues her legacy of mentoring collegiate athletes by managing physiological, emotional, and strength development programming for sports teams and local universities across Southern California.

Guerra enjoys an elite and loyal client roster which includes: ONE Championship's two-sport World Champion Janet Todd, NBA superstars Blake Griffin, Deondre Jordan and James Harden as well as other NBA stars; West Coast MMA fighters; Domestic and international Tennis, Volleyball, Soccer Professionals, and Division 1 Collegiate athletes at universities including Stanford, Duke, Cal Berkeley, University of Washington and Harvard. In 2017, Guerra expanded the West Coast headquarters for Game Ready Performance (GRP), the Athletic Engineering company she founded in 2012. As Founder & Head Physiologist at GRP, Guerra and her team service 300+ elite youth, collegiate and professional athletes per week from their 3,200 sq. ft. indoor/outdoor Athletic Engineering and Recovery Lab in Hermosa Beach, California.

From The Eye of Ayahuasca is Jackie Guerra's first poetry collection exploring the healing power of the Indigenous practice of Ayahuasca from the Ashaninka people of Peru in the Mayantuyacu lineage of Maestro Juan Flores Salazar.

She is currently working on her first music album that is a product of the plant medicine voice. Her two singles, Energia Positiva, which speaks to the power of positive energy. The second song is History in the Making, speaking to the power of coming together to heal the earth and ourselves.

When she is not training her clients, you can find her hanging with her dog Paula, her bird Sun Szu and her two tortoises Luna and Lakshmi.

She lives in Hermosa Beach enjoying the Southern California ocean vibes.

Lear more at:

www.ingramcontent.com/pod-product-compliance
Lightning Source LLC
Chambersburg PA
CBHW051301120626
46547CB00015B/2041